Captivated by the Master

Also by Fr. Brian Mullady, O.P.
from EWTN Publishing:

The Decalogue Decoded

Fr. Brian Thomas Becket Mullady, O.P., S.T.D.

Captivated by the Master

A Theological Consideration of Jesus Christ

EWTN PUBLISHING, INC.

Irondale, Alabama

EWTN Publishing, Inc.
5817 Old Leeds Road, Irondale, AL 35210

Distributed by Sophia Institute Press, Box 5284, Manchester, NH 03108.

paperback ISBN 978-1-68278-132-6

ebook ISBN 978-1-68278-133-3

Library of Congress Control Number: 2020938400

To Fr. Christopher Fadok
and the Friars of the Western Dominican Province

Contents

Introduction 3

1. In the Beginning 7

2. Jesus Makes Sense .19

3. Heresies 31

4. Christ in the Creeds 41

5. Full of Grace 51

6. Full of Truth 61

7. Jesus the "Imperfect"? 73

8. He Wills It 83

9. The Early Years 93

10. The Public Ministry 105

11. *Kenosis* and the Cross 115

12. He Is Risen 127

13. The Savior Is Exalted 137

About the Author 147

Captivated by the Master

Introduction

The English author Dorothy Sayers wrote a series of plays in the 1930s based on the Gospels. In response, many young people came to her and asked where she got the profound and beautiful ideas about Christ that she portrayed in her drama. She answered that she hadn't invented anything new: one can find them in the early Church councils, such as Nicaea, Ephesus, and Chalcedon. The problem was that, at that time in the Anglican Church, clergy were de-emphasizing doctrine and tradition in favor of faddish social justice, and so beautiful doctrinal truths about Jesus seemed new and fresh.

This way of thinking, of course, isn't isolated to the distant past. At a seminary where I taught in the early nineties, the students were required to do pastoral work teaching religion in local parishes. Many of the directors of religious education told them not to teach doctrine, but to focus on just making the children feel happy to be there. It's no surprise, then, that our Church today is dealing with almost three generations of uncatechized adults. It's also no wonder that more and more people are rejecting organized religion in general, and the Church in particular.

Sayers believed that many reject Christianity, as G.K. Chesterton famously observed, without having a clue what the Church has always taught. This is very true when it comes to Who Christ is and what He has done. Sayers wrote an article to answer this problem, which was published as "The Dogma Is the Drama." This is the bottom line to the present book: the dogma is the drama.

Why write another book on Christ? This book attempts to address a gap in the knowledge of modern Christians about the nature and implications of the traditional, systematic doctrine of Christ. One could, of course, take a semester course in Christology at a seminary or university, but many people simply do not have the resources to do this. It seems fitting, therefore, to provide a short summary of the traditional teaching of the Catholic Church on Christ for the training and consolation of the faithful. The nature of the union between God and man in Christ was slowly defined over 500 years by several major councils of the Church. The examination of this definition may seem tedious at times, but clarity is a necessary foundation for understanding why Christ came to earth and how the nature He assumed promoted His purpose, which was to redeem the human race. Modern attempts to separate Christ from His Cross and to suggest that His purpose was merely to resist unjust social structures or to be a wise moral teacher are not only misplaced but simply false. Beyond their falseness, they destroy the uniqueness and drama of the Christian message. On these accounts, one does not adore Jesus as God, but as a role model or guru. This is the result of the Enlightenment, which denied the possibility of miracles and taught that human reason could save mankind. In this light, the only way to understand the undeniable goodness of Jesus is purely humanistic and materialist: He was just a good reasoner, just an effective leader. Grace is neither touched nor taught.

Thus we end up with an assumed distinction between what the apostles *actually experienced* in their relationship with Christ and what the Church has abstractly taught about Him: the Jesus of history and the Jesus of faith. The former is a Christology from below with no place for miracle, metaphysics, or grace; the latter is a Christology from above that exhibits all these things, but only as a historical and academic curiosity, with no implications for daily life and ethics.

The new Christology, of course, affects how one interprets the Scriptures, which is the true account, inspired by God, of what Jesus did and taught. A flawed understanding of Christ leads to a flawed interpretation of these accounts, with miracles discounted and uncomfortable sacrifices reimagined. For example, the multiplication of the loaves becomes the miracle of sharing, where it is assumed (with no textual evidence) that the only thing Christ did was shame the crowds into distributing food they had hidden. Worse, the Crucifixion becomes an unfortunate incident rather than the central act of Christ's mission, and the Resurrection becomes a fabrication of the faith community rather than the consummation of God's salvific work.

A flawed Christology makes Christianity senseless. If we are to imitate Christ, we have to know and love Who He *really* is, not some modern, comfortable reimagining that's usually reducible to "niceness." On this account, grace is no longer a supernatural gift that elevates our prayer life so we can know as God knows and love as He loves, but simply an encouragement to be nice. Human problems, then, are solved only with better bureaucracies and more compelling inducements to niceness, rather than through a personal relationship with Christ Who actually elevates our souls, not just our feelings or our pocketbooks.

When we get Christ wrong, the God of man becomes man, and Jesus just shows us how to be more human. Sin and redemption become too negative to have any place in genuine faith; and the Church is reduced to a human society and the sacraments to celebrations of ourselves. Finally, the Eucharist becomes an assembly where the community gathers to find unity in itself and Christ-as-guru, rather than communion with God and Christ-as-God.

In other words, getting the details of Christ's identity and natures wrong is fundamental to so many of the problems we see today in the Church and in the world. Dorothy Sayers ended her article on religion without drama thus: "Wilt Thou be baptized in this faith?" Her answer: "No fear!"

—Fr. Brian Mullady, O.P.
Monday of the Octave of Easter 2020

1

In the Beginning

Who is Jesus Christ?

It seems like a simple question. He's the Messiah, the second Person of the Trinity, the subject of the Gospels. At every Mass we hear about Him in the Liturgy of the Word, and He is made present to us in the Liturgy of the Eucharist. We see Him on crucifixes, icons, and even television. Even in a secular age, He is one of the most visible persons in our society.

But all that only gets us so far—and in some cases only raises more questions than answers. What does it *mean* to be the Messiah, to be the second Person of the Trinity, to be the focal point of all of Scripture? What does it *mean* to be the Word and to be the Blessed Sacrament? And what errors and misperceptions about Jesus are hidden in the representation of Him in our culture?

These aren't idle questions. Understanding Christ is essential to understanding what it means to be a human person—specifically what it means to be a person in relationship with God. In other words, it's essential to living our faith to the fullest.

But in order to come to know the true Christ better, we first have to cut through the lies and misconceptions we see all around us about Jesus Christ. For example, a few years ago a Catholic newspaper reported that a priest had stated in a homily that Jesus misinterpreted a psalm that He quoted in the Gospel. When questioned on how we can trust what Christ says if He can be wrong about things such as the interpretation of a psalm, the priest responded: "You've got to remember, Jesus didn't have the benefit of the same religious education that we have today, with all the things that modern scholarship brings us."[1] Apparently, if Jesus had gotten His seminary education in 1990 He would be much wiser.

Cardinal Joseph Ratzinger, who went on to become Pope Benedict XVI, gave a talk to European theologians in 1989, called "Difficulties Confronting the Faith in Europe Today." In this talk, he stated that Catholic theology is in trouble in three basic areas. The first was what he called "the metaphysics of creation." In other words, a number of teachers of the Catholic faith today simply do not believe in a transcendent God Who created everything. The second was the afterlife. He said he heard a preacher at Mass try to convince his congregation there was no hell, then no purgatory, and finally no heaven. Rather, the ideal to which we should dedicate ourselves is just better social structures.

These converge on a third area, according to Ratzinger: Who is Christ? At the time, he said that people reduce Christ to a political liberator or a good middle-class person who never challenges us and who teaches us only how to be nice. The trouble with both of these models is that they rob Christ of the principal reason He came from heaven to earth: to die on the Cross for us. These modernists want a Christianity and a Christ without a Cross. So, it seems an urgent effort at clarification is now needed.

Let's begin, naturally, with Scripture:

> But when the time had fully come, God sent forth his Son, born of woman, born under the law, to redeem those who were under the law, so that we might receive adoption as

---

[1] Father Brian Mullady, O.P., "Jesus Christ Our Savior," *National Catholic Register*, July 22, 1990.

sons. And because you are sons, God has sent the Spirit of his Son into our hearts, crying, "Abba! Father!" (Gal. 4:4–6)

This short text summarizes the basic points of Catholic doctrine concerning Christ the Lord. First, Christ was sent by God and is *the* Son of God, not merely *a* son of God; thus He is within the Trinity and existed before His birth in time. Second, Jesus was sent in the fullness of time, which means that while He existed outside of time, He also actually existed and acted within history when He took to Himself a human nature. Third, He was born under the law, exemplifying our need for redemption. Fourth, He was born of a woman, demonstrating that He was a human being like us in all things—except, of course, sin. Finally, as both a Person of the Trinity and a human being He was and is a channel bringing the divine life of the Holy Spirit to us, allowing us to enter totally into the mystery of the Blessed Trinity.

This is a complex, beautiful, powerful view of Christ—and it contrasts sharply with a modern view. A modern picture of Christ, as we've suggested, goes something like this: "He was a good man. In fact, he was so good that he might somehow be identified with God. (How exactly isn't clear.) He preached a simple doctrine of love and pacifism. He was basically a kind and peaceful person." In modern interpretation there is a serious conflict between the Jesus defined by faith in the Creed and the Jesus of history, who was just a nice person who was given certain extraordinary godlike gifts. His miracles, then, are explained or dismissed as merely hopeful projections of the faith of the community—up to and including His Resurrection.

Thus the Jesus of faith and the Jesus of history are placed in irreconcilable conflict. Some proclaim tremendous truths in the Creed, and then act as though Christ was ignorant of His mission and only came to it after a long period of self-searching—perhaps not even understanding His own Resurrection. Further, in portrayals such as *The Last Temptation of Christ*, Jesus is shown to have truly suffered internal temptation to sin. Martin Scorsese can say that he wasn't trying to reproduce the Gospels, and we may well believe him. But the trouble is, there are so many Christians today who basically accept this view! Many people want to reduce Christ to a human being as ignorant and weak as anyone else, I suppose in order to make Him "approachable."

Still others like to think that Jesus was a political revolutionary, and that the Gospels are primarily political statements. Some are more specific, arguing that Christ was a member of a particular faction, the Zealots, who wanted to liberate Israel from Rome by armed conflict. Here we find a Christ Who is more interested in, and suffers for, earthly troubles. Again, it defines Jesus down to our level, comparing Him to other particularly well-regarded men, such as Martin Luther King, Jr. or Mahatma Gandhi.

This type of thinking erases everything supernatural or godly or Trinitarian about Jesus Christ. If we subscribe to these views, we not only deny His divinity, but our own divine dignity and calling. Why did Christ suffer death on the Cross? Was it because it was necessary, in obedience to the will of His Father, so that He could reverse sin and death? This hard but beautiful truth is wiped away in the modern, comfortable retelling. (Some even *blame* Christ, suggesting the reason Jesus had to suffer was that He wasn't pluralistic and understanding enough. Heresy upon heresy.)

In other modern movements, we find the idea that Christ is something like a spiritual life force within us. People will even say that they and others are Christ — not in the sense that they are conformed to Him by grace, but in the sense that anyone who is kind and gentle is a kind of Christ. This completely destroys the uniqueness of Jesus. On this understanding, Christianity has nothing to do with any kind of deep inner sense of loss of God that demands resolution by an obedient Savior; it's just about discovering how to be a smiling face to everyone and in every place.

Now, I have nothing against being happy or friendly! The problem is that this kind of religion is superficial and easily disconnected from truth—deep truths about heaven and Earth, humanity and salvation. Some who teach this kind of doctrine say that the Gospels are just like reading a newspaper. How sad! They see nothing metaphysical, nothing philosophical, nothing beyond the ordinary about interpreting them. But then, we have to ask: What's the point? If they're just interesting accounts of an interesting historical person, they can be reserved for classrooms. There's no need to *live* by them.

Another way of dividing the Jesus of faith from the Jesus of history is by separating the doctrinal Christ from the Christ experienced and loved by the apostles. The modern way of looking at Christ has a great deal of difficulty explaining how the Creed relates to the experience of the apostles because, again, it lowers Christ to our level. And so proponents of this view reduce the Gospels to something like cocktail-party conversation—full of intrigue but empty of meaning. They take all the punch out of the Gospels; they don't want Jesus to lead to any deep interior formation or repentance. The result is Christ as bourgeois moralist, speaking comforting nothings that make humans feel safe.

Altogether, what the modern Christology gives us is a Christ without divinity and a Christ without the Cross. This is directly opposed to Scripture, the liturgy, and the doctrine of the Church. In the Easter liturgy, for instance, we say, "O happy fault. O necessary sin of Adam that bore for us so great a Redeemer!" In other words, we cannot understand Christ's coming unless we understand sin. To understand the Redeemer, we have to understand what we're being redeemed from.

Let's start right at the beginning with Adam, the first and most perfect human being until the coming of Christ. He was perfect because he had all the powers of man and an inner order of soul because he was created in God's grace and thus without sin. What Adam shows us is that the original reason man was created was that he, and all of creation, might be centered around and ordered toward God. Creation exists for the sake of man, but the perfection of man is found in and through God, Who is other than the world. We all have this destiny: to know and to love God in His fullness.

And in order to move ourselves toward that full and perfect knowledge of God while we are here on earth, we have to desire Him. That desire is the product of love — not just a vague feeling of affection for God, but a life ordered to His glory. Finally, in order to love the Trinity fully, as a friend, we have to be elevated to the Trinity's level. And of course, we cannot do this on our own; God Himself has to enter into us and elevate us to that level by giving us grace. This is the work of Jesus Christ and His Church.

We could say, then, that justification consists primarily in the Holy Trinity elevating us to the level of God interiorly — that is, it consists in the presence of the Holy Spirit within our souls. Adam enjoyed this before the sin, but after the sin he lost it. Christ restores us to this justification; it is in Him alone that we can find integrity and wholeness, because only when we have a friendship with the Holy Trinity is it possible for us to desire the full vision of God and to move actively toward it.

Now, to be lost in original sin, as followers of God were before Christ, isn't to be totally depraved. We each always have an intellect, a will, emotions, and a body, all given to us by God. We can still respond to God's call with our intellects and wills, even when our souls are sick, just as a sick body can still be active and do good work. The trouble is that we can't keep it up. Intimate knowledge of the Holy Trinity isn't just God overlooking sin from the outside, but the internal elevation of our souls to His friendship.

This friendship was granted to Adam before the sin because Adam himself was created in grace.

This means that because God wished to share interior friendship with Adam, He elevated the powerful gifts of intellect and will and so on to a perfect integrity. Among other things, the intellect had a perfect contemplative knowledge. You could say Adam was always in the state of infused contemplation, always present to the Trinity. Second, Adam's will was continuously and spontaneously responsive to the will of God. Third, Adam enjoyed total integrity in his emotions, eagerly and willingly seeking to obey God's law concerning him and the world. Finally, by a kind of external protection, God freed Adam from sickness and from death, keeping him from experiencing anything that might compromise this beautiful integrity of body and soul.

But in order to maintain this condition, Adam had to rely upon God for his inner sanctification, what we call sanctifying grace. Sanctifying grace is a true change in the soul whereby man is elevated to communion and friendship with God. However, in order to persevere in that supernatural internal integrity, Adam also had what we call actual grace. Actual grace is not a change within the soul, but God's help to enlighten the intellect and strengthen the will to perform each act from a divine and eternal point of view. In other words, even though Adam had this perfect and harmonious integrity within him, he had to rely on God to preserve it.

God aided Adam as long as he gladly received of this gift of integrity. That is, these gifts depended on Adam's love and obedience, existing as long as he was in the state of grace. In that state, Adam and Eve had an easy virtue produced by grace, but to persevere in that virtue they had to depend on God. God wants us to enjoy His friendship in equality with Him, yet He does not desire us to pridefully grasp at that goal, but rather to receive it graciously. In the original sin, Adam and Eve questioned this gift, relying on their own powers rather than God's, and lost it. They made a choice without relying on God to enlighten them, rejecting love and obedience, sinning first in mind and then in deed.

Once man sinned, he not only lost grace but also lost the special gifts he had received: spontaneous obedience, infused knowledge, easy virtue, and freedom from suffering and death. This original sin is the source of our alienation from ourselves, from the world, and from God. We can see this in Adam's immediate shame, hiding himself from his God. The world of Eden, in which Adam was at peace with nature, became a hostile and threatening place.

Importantly, people became alienated from one another first in marriage. Adam and Eve were initially perfectly loving and giving, so they could be naked and not ashamed. The body was a means of unselfish self-giving. They experienced creation and existence as a beautiful gift from God. Then, after the sin, humanity experienced the possibility of manipulation and deceit, each person suspicious of the other's motives and aims.

Since the sin, people have sought to find in earthly things the complete interior peace once experienced through union with God. But these can never suffice. After the sin, the first children adopt this utilitarian attitude, and in jealousy Cain slays Abel. The earth itself rebels against man wounded by selfish egotism and resists cultivation. Work existed before the sin, but it was a joy; now it is toil and brings forth uneven results, including thorns and thistles. Childbearing becomes an occasion of intense pain for a woman, and husband and wife seek to rule rather than serve each other. This is all the dread fruit of the first denial of the gift of grace.

But God does not leave the human race bereft in this condition. In the state of grace and integrity, He brings forth a greater mercy than even the original creation of Adam and Eve. Man was destined for union with God before the sin and now God promises to resolve our alienation through a miracle: the union of the human race with God in person. It is alienation from which Christ wishes to redeem us.

God promises this Redeemer in His words to Satan: "I will put enmity between you and the woman, and between your seed and her seed; he shall bruise your head, and you will bruise his heel" (Gen. 3:15). Who is Christ? Above all, He is a Redeemer.

2

Jesus Makes Sense

Why did the Son of God become a human being? What reasonability can we find in the Incarnation?

In the first chapter, we discussed the reality of sin as alienation from God in order to understand the reality of Jesus as Redeemer. His Incarnation was not arbitrary, but essential to God's plan to restore us to His friendship. We can see the perfection of that friendship in Adam, whom the Lord created in grace. Adam was at peace with himself, with creation, and with others because he was at peace with God due to the presence of the Holy Spirit within him. God elevated Adam and all of his powers so that his choices would always be in conformity with the will of God.

St. John Henry Newman pointed out that the only correct and complete point of view is that of God from eternity:

> There are ten thousand ways of looking at this world, but only one right way. The man of pleasure has his way, the man of gain his, and the man of intellect his.... Each has his own way of looking at the things which come before him, and each has a wrong way. There is but one right way; it is the way in which God looks at the world. Aim at looking at it in God's way. Aim at seeing things as God sees them.[2]

---

[2] *Parochial and Plain Sermons*, vol. 5, *Unreal Words* (London: Rivingtons, 1869), 44.

Adam and Eve were called upon to look at the world as God does, and they were able to do so because they had *sanctifying grace*, and they were able to persevere in doing so because they had *actual grace*. They were different from beasts because they could choose their actions; they knew who they were and knew the difference between themselves and the rest of creation, and thus could be partners with God in realizing their own destiny. In other words, they demonstrated their union with God by their obedience to His Word.

Enter the tempter. Satan's strategy is to try to divide Adam and Eve from their very selves and from their destiny. He's very crafty: He doesn't deny the existence of God but suggests that it's *God's* laws that alienate man from himself. He suggests that God's existence is in conflict with the freedom of the human will. This is a great lie — perhaps *the* great lie. For when we look at the world from God's point of view, we can see that doing His will is what freedom is all about. Freedom and truth are inextricably linked. By questioning the gift of harmonious integrity and protection he enjoyed from God, Adam made a movement of his will against obedience and against the all-giving spirit of God. Thus sin entered the world. When Adam disobeyed, he acted against the union of love that should have cemented him with God, and as a result he lost God's internal and external guidance. The sin was committed in both the intellect and the will, and so the fault is in both — and the punishments for the sin correspond to the fault.

The first punishment to enter the human race on account of the original sin was the darkening of the intellect. We became unable to appreciate why we were truly here — why we existed at all, what our purpose was. Second, our wills were weakened and infected with malice. Our nature wasn't and isn't totally depraved, but we do have a tendency to want to dance to our own tune and to make the rules ourselves. Third, we lost control of our emotions, which are properly subservient to reason. The feeling of love, for instance, goes this way and that way, and there's no unity or harmony or integrity in our love. We hate what we should love, and we love what we should hate.

> For I do not do the good I want, but the evil I do not want is what I do.... For I delight in the law of God, in my inmost self, but I see in my members another law at war with the law of my mind and making me captive to the law of sin which dwells in my members. (Rom. 7:19, 22–23)

And finally, as St. Paul implies here, in the body we lost the perfect integrity between our desires and our body's responses to the world. Matter tends to corrupt, and the body tends to corruption, and to death.

Thus Adam, who had been accustomed to the integrity of grace, suddenly experienced that his mind and will and emotions and body were in disarray. He was confused and afraid and embarrassed; he was divided within himself, and he didn't know what to do. Because he had lost his union with God and thus his justification, he was uneasy, even ashamed at the fact of his own existence, and so he hid himself. He was also morally and emotionally alienated from his wife, and so they had to sew fig leaves together because they were afraid of being manipulated by each other.

They weren't at peace anymore — in themselves, with God, or with one another. This passed down to the children, brother against brother, and Cain killed Abel. The sin spread its punishment throughout the whole human race. At Babel, the very language we use, which is a sign of our difference from animals and of our rationality, became a source of confusion and alienation.

The final sign of the original sin, then, is the alienation we experience from the material world itself. We who should dominate the material world because we are *embodied spirits* are now dominated by it. In other words, we die: ashes to ashes and dust to dust. But God doesn't leave us bereft in this condition. No, here we find the most astounding and yet reasonable solution to the alienation of the human race. And here we also find the answer to the age-old question of why God allowed us to fall into sin.

It's easy to think that if we hadn't sinned, everything would have been fine. We wouldn't have had to suffer anything. There would have been no reason for us to experience difficulties in life. Maybe, we are tempted to think, God couldn't really be good if He allowed us to sin. The goodness of God cannot be seen in allowing the fault and applying the punishment.

But this is the most beautiful truth of the Christian religion, and the reality that sets it apart from all non-Christian creeds: God allowed us to sin so that He might show more goodness and love to us, so that He might raise a being to Himself who was disintegrated, so that He might prove Himself a divine physician, and so that He might, in doing so, give us the greatest miracle that could ever exist: that God in person could become one of the human race.

Now, some have said that Christ would have become incarnate whether we needed a redeemer or not, simply out of God's love for humanity. It's certainly true that Christ *could have* taken flesh regardless of the sin; it certainly wouldn't have been outside His power. But it would have been outside His *justice*. There would have been no *reason* why God should submit to such humiliation — the humiliation of our limits, of our mortality. St. Paul said that Christ Jesus,

> though he was in the form of God, did not count equality with God a thing to be grasped, but emptied himself, taking the form of a servant, being born in the likeness of men. And being found in human form he humbled himself and became obedient unto death, even death on a cross. (Phil. 2:6–8)

There's no reason that God would have done this except out of love *to free us from our sins*. That's what the whole Christian tradition teaches us. Christ came to atone for both our fault and our punishment, and He had to address each.

The atonement then has a twofold character that is central to the doctrine of Christ. First, atonement demands that justice be restored in the face of a sin — disobedience to the Creator — that was committed in both the intellect and the will. The evil of punishment, including the loss of grace and the special gifts given to the human race by God, resulted from it. In place of infused knowledge, the human race experienced ignorance; in place of loving obedience in the will, rebellion; in place of the easy virtue of ordered passions, concupiscence; in place of divine protection of the body, suffering and death. Jesus took flesh to atone for the sin of disobedience, so it would be unfitting for Him to assume any punishment that would compromise His perfect obedience in love. He could only assume suffering and death. To satisfy for sin, Christ takes on human flesh so that in His human will and His human mind and in His human emotions and body He may make satisfaction for our disobedience by His obedience.

The second aspect of the atoning work of the Incarnation is as a cure for our sin and its resulting punishment. Sin extinguishes the presence of the Holy Spirit in the soul, which is necessary for man to arrive at his destiny: the vision of God in heaven. Christ restores us by sending the Holy Spirit, along with His own presence, to dwell within our hearts again. This is the essential cure for the sinfulness of mankind as a whole, and of each of us individually.

By a sin of *disobedience* we became divided from ourselves; God became incarnate so that by *obedience* He Who was without fault might satisfy for our fault, and for the punishments for our sin. Of all the punishments that Christ could have assumed for us, there was only one — our mortality — that would not have threatened

His ability to be obedient to the Father. He couldn't take upon Himself ignorance or malice or interior temptation. But He could, and had to, take upon Himself suffering and death because these do not have to do with moral weaknesses with respect to God. He did this by lovingly obeying on the Cross to atone for the unloving disobedience of Adam and Eve. His obedience atones for their fault.

And so the Incarnation *makes sense*. God could have, with His absolute power, redeemed us simply by saying so, but that would have been a denial of His justice. Thus, when we examine all the ways that God could have redeemed us, the one that makes the most sense is that He should take on flesh. Through the obedience of Christ He could atone for the original sin and reintroduce us into the divine life that we lost through the disobedience of Adam.

The Incarnation also has reasonability as an incentive to the life of faith and virtue. God chose to resolve man's sin as He did as an encouragement to faith, hope, charity, and courage — to show that Satan has no real power over us if we rely on God. When we see our God made visible, we have a greater assurance of what we believe about Him, because it comes directly from Him!

The Incarnation also teaches and leads us to hope in God because, when we see all that God suffered for us, it should sustain us in perseverance. When we are tempted to give up hope, we can meditate on Christ's agony in the Garden. If we're without friends, we can remember that Jesus was deserted by His friends. If we're suffering in our body, we can recall how painful the wounds of Christ were. If our reputation has been destroyed, we can think of all the people who attacked Christ's reputation throughout His ministry.

The Incarnation is also a motive for charity — that is, love of God. We can see that God's lowering Himself was done without force because, of course, God can't be forced. He did none of this out of self-interest. He didn't receive anything from becoming incarnate; we received everything. He did it out of pure love for us, even though we may not have been terribly lovable, at least as individuals.

Christ's taking flesh should also spur us to right action. He was a living example of what the life of goodness and virtue looks like. Christ showed us what it means to live spiritually, to disregard and overcome the desires of the flesh. He showed us the dignity of human nature: that we are called to life in the Blessed Trinity.

He also gives us an example to deliver us from evil. Christ's Incarnation is a refutation of presumption: It wasn't that God foresaw that Christ would be so good, and therefore gave Him grace. No, the action and decision belonged only to God: Christ was good not because of some preexisting merits but because He received the grace of the Incarnation to begin with. Thus it is also a remedy for our pride: If Jesus didn't aim to demonstrate or achieve divinity *even though He was in fact divine*, then how much more should we embrace humility? His life in the flesh teaches us not to be ruled by desire.

The Incarnation shows us what the fullness of freedom is: freedom from sin, not moral bondage or the psychological bondage of soul. Human freedom is found in the sheer goodness of the human will filled with God.

Christ, as a good physician, also wanted to give us an example of forgiveness. He forgave all those who crucified Him, including us, whose sins merit such punishment. He knew that all of us at some point would have unresolved anger at others, and that all our attempts at reconciliation would be spurned. Even if we have a mature and Christian anger regarding a genuine evil that has been perpetrated against us, if we are guided by God's forgiveness then we can be set free from the bondage of anger and hatred toward those who have wronged us.

Christ therefore assumes human nature to destroy all sinfulness and to join us back to God, thus affirming the Father's justice and mercy. In order to do this, both His divine and human natures must remain intact. In theology we say that Christ became hypostatically (more on this in a later chapter) united to human nature. The Nicene Creed states He is "true God and true man"; we might say that He is "altogether God and altogether man." He must be God because the nature of the first sin was against God; He must be man because only someone from the race of Adam could actually atone for both fault and punishment.

Again, this doesn't imply that any course of action was *necessary* for God; no one and nothing can constrain Him. It demonstrates that the Incarnation, a mystery without complete explanation, is not arbitrary, but corresponds to justice. It also shows that Christ assumed His human nature freely and fittingly. For the atonement to be fitting, the union of divine and human natures in Christ cannot compromise either, and so the union did not occur in the natures themselves but in the Person of the Word. We'll talk about this in more detail later, but for now let us simply say that the principle of humanity and the principle of divinity were both fully present in Christ.

We are tempted to say that, in the Incarnation, Christ just came down from heaven. But that's not quite right. It's more complete to say that He elevated human nature to Himself, so that when we see Christ in the flesh we see the person of God Himself. This nature can never be lost: We can lose that union by sin, but Christ could not.

Could Christ have become an angel or an animal? In God's absolute power, one must answer yes. But this would compromise the logic of His atonement. Could all three of the Persons of the Trinity become Incarnate? Of course. But it is most fitting to the Word. The Word is the one in Whom the universe is ordered to

God, because in Him all things were made. The Word brings us to participate in life like a son, for the Word is the only-begotten Son of the Father even as God in His divine nature.

What sense is there in the Incarnation, then? In Him, we see our God made visible, and so we are caught up in love of the God we cannot see. Thomas Aquinas always speaks about the fittingness of the Incarnation. By this he means that there is more truth we can discover in this choice of God than in any other we can think of. But the final reason can never be completely understood. It is a mystery hidden in God but delightful to contemplate. The medieval theologians used to call it the *miraculum miraculorum* (the miracle of miracles): The person of the Word took flesh that it might be an instrument of His divinity. Thus He became a channel by which—by Whom—we who had been divided might return to the integrity of grace.

The redemption, therefore, requires Christ not give up being a Divine Person, but rather that He assume a further human nature, shared with Adam. If He were only a human person, He could not repair our fallen nature as the one high priest. There is only one "I," one Person, in Jesus of Nazareth Who can be born, know, love, weep, work, change, and die. And that "I" is God, the Person of the Word.

And so the Incarnation can be defined as the assumption of a human nature—an ordered composition of body and soul—by a Divine Person without confusing them with His divine nature. All errors, and we shall see many in the next chapter, can be reduced to the negation of these two natures, or of the unity of the Person in Christ.

3

Heresies

From the very beginning, the Church's understanding of Christ's human and divine nature has been challenged by Christological heresies. We've already talked about how moderns have misinterpreted Christ and how the Incarnation is genuinely and completely reasonable, even as it always remains a mystery. Now let's look at ancient and enduring errors regarding Christ. There are several points that must be clarified: the Incarnation must involve no change in God; Christ must be God; and the dual natures of Christ cannot be compromised.

The Incarnation, rightly understood, is Christ as a Divine Person — that is, a person Who always existed with the divine nature as the Word of God — taking flesh and assuming a human nature, which includes an ordered composition of body and soul. This isn't easy, and it's very mysterious. Throughout history there have been people who have tried to contrive their own explanations of Christ and, in so doing, have denied one or another part of this mystery. Usually the errors concerning the Incarnation have to do with the fact that Christ is *begotten*. What do we mean by this word? In our liturgy, we have three ways we speak of Christ being begotten in the opening prayers for the three Masses of Christmas Day. Here the liturgy can demonstrate theology.

In the Mass at midnight the entrance antiphon comes from Psalm 2:7: "The Lord said to me: You are my Son. It is I who have begotten you this day." This begetting doesn't refer to a begetting in time—that is, to Christ's birth by the Virgin Mary. Rather, this refers to the begetting of the Word in the Trinity at the beginning of time. The Word Who is coequal with the Father was *eternally* begotten by Him. The words "this day" in the psalm mean the eternal day of the Lord, of which Christmas is a reflection in time. We who are in time enter into the eternal union of the Father and the Word in the Holy Spirit by the grace of the Incarnation.

In the second Mass of Christmas, at dawn, we hear in Isaiah 9: "Today a light will shine upon us, for the Lord is born for us." This refers to the begetting that occurred in the womb of the Blessed Virgin Mary, when the eternally begotten God took on a new way of existing, a new relationship with creation. The same Person Who already shared a communion of Persons with the Holy Trinity could now also act in time, knowing and loving and suffering in a human way. Notice that God is not changed, but nature is changed. All of us are called to be united to God in this nature. In Christ, creation is united to God in His Person.

Finally, in the Mass during the day the opening prayer also comes from Isaiah 9: "A child is born for us, and a son is given to us; his scepter of power rests upon his shoulder, and his name will be called Messenger of great counsel." This refers to the begetting of Christ *in us*, where He is brought forth to us so that He might dwell in us. Mary presents Him to us so that we might perceive the glory of God in the humility of Christ. The preface to the Eucharistic Prayer for the Christmas Mass says it very beautifully: "In him we see our God made visible and so are caught up in love of the God we cannot see." And so there is no diluting of the divine nature in the Incarnation. What Christ takes upon Himself as a Divine Person is a *new and different nature* that gives Him a new way He can act with and for us. Jesus is not just another sinful human person who was given a special grace by God; He is the Divine Person with the divine nature Who, by a special grace, assumed a human nature and acted through that human nature as a tool of His divinity.

Now let us turn to some of the notable ways thinkers and groups have been mistaken about this doctrine in ways that compromise Christ's Redemption. These errors aren't that hard to fall into, given the complexity of the mystery, which is why the early Church promulgated very explicit definitions about Christ's dual nature. There are certain characteristics these heresies share with one another. The most important one is that almost every heretic affirms *something true* about Christ, but does so in a disproportionate or exaggerated way such that it denies something else true about Him.

These heresies have three basic problems. First, they deny Christ's divinity by affirming that He was only a human person and so was an adopted son of God, in which case it becomes difficult to see how He could possibly reveal the Holy Spirit to us or in justice atone to God for our sin. Second, they deny His humanity by saying it was only an illusion, in which case Christ couldn't really be obedient in our place because He would have shared nothing with us and couldn't atone for our disobedience. Third, they make a more difficult error, saying that Christ was neither fully God nor fully man but a kind of monster or hybrid, leaving Him unable to fulfill either His divine or human calling.

Let's start with the heresy of Photinus, who was what we call an "adoptionist." He held that Jesus Christ was an adopted son of God like the rest of us, and thus did not exist even as a Divine Person before His conception in His mother's womb. Photinus taught that Christ *earned* the glory of His divinity, as a man, by His suffering. In other words, the union of Christ with God was not peculiar to Him, but available to anyone who so sacrificed—a saint among other saints, a prophet among other prophets. We say in the Creed that Christ came down from heaven; Photinus held that He only went *up* to heaven. So the adoptionist heresy teaches that there is one person in Christ, a human person who earned a divine nature.

Next there's Nestorius, who was actually the patriarch of Constantinople. He reacted against the adoptionist heresy but went too far, asserting that there were actually two persons in Christ with two *totally separate* natures. How does Christ, as God, dwell in man? He does so, according to Nestorius, as a man would dwell in his clothing: He donned humanity like a coat, but that humanity was never integrated into Him.

How did Nestorius come to teach this? In the year 428, he was asked to pronounce on the suitability of a Greek term when applied to the Blessed Virgin: *Theotokos*, which means "God-bearer." His reply shows that even hierarchs are not free from doctrinal difficulties. He said *anthropotokos*, "bearer of man," and *christokos*, "bearer of Christ," were better, and that one could not apply *theotokos* to Mary. Of course, Mary could not give birth to a divine nature, but she could give birth to a Divine Person with a second human nature, and in that sense the term *Theotokos* can be applied to her. Nestorius denied this, and thus denied Christ's *integrally* divine nature.

Here we see a characteristic of all Christian heresies. In saying that Mary was the bearer of Christ *as a man*, Nestorius was saying something true. But his terms weren't precise about whether Christ is *also* God. A person could affirm Nestorius's definition and still deny that Christ is God — and that's exactly what Nestorius did, holding Christ's divine and human natures, God and man, to be completely separate. He was so interested — and rightly so! — in affirming the absolute divinity and the absolute humanity of Christ that he actually created two wholly distinct centers of existence. Christ could not become flesh in His divinity, Nestorius held, because God cannot take flesh and have a genuinely human life. But that meant there could be no real communion between the two, thus compromising what the Incarnation was all about. So his heresy affirms there are not only two natures, but two persons in Christ. In fact, many think that the Islamic prophet Mohammed was greatly influenced by a Nestorian.

Arius, the most famous and influential Christological heretic, reacted against both of these ideas. Arius was a deacon and then a priest, and he had a very austere and grave manner. He had a flexible and subtle intellect, and his eloquence persuaded many people of his errors. Arius argued that there was only *one person* and *one nature* in Christ, and that *both of these* were created. This has implications for the Trinity: he taught that the Word even in the Trinity had to be created, even though this couldn't logically be, because he was overly invested in affirming the uniqueness of God.

This meant the Christ was not God in any accepted sense of the word, because He had a beginning. There was a time, according to Arius, that the Word did not exist. (In fact his followers developed something of a chant or a taunt: "There was a time when He was not!") There was a time when Jesus did not exist—not just Jesus incarnate, Who came into being in Mary's womb, but Jesus the second Person of the Blessed Trinity. Of course, this is not what either the Scriptures or the orthodox faith teach. It's right there at the beginning of John's Gospel:

> In the beginning was the Word, and the Word was with God, and the Word was God. He was in the beginning with God; all things were made through him, and without him was not anything made that was made. In him was life, and the life was the light of men. The light shines in the darkness, and the darkness has not overcome it. (John 1:1–5)

Arius's teaching, in contrast, meant that the Word was not coequal to God and thus that, as man, Jesus had no direct intimate communion with God. He had no direct knowledge of the Father. He was a kind of half-god: not simply a creature but the greatest of the creatures, and also not one with God Himself. Jesus was the most perfect of created beings, but still created. Because Arius's Christ was not eternal, He was liable to change — and that meant it was possible for Him to sin. He didn't receive a special grace at His Incarnation; God merely foresaw, as in the adoptionist heresy, that He was going to be incredibly virtuous, therefore God rewarded Him with the grace that allowed Jesus to be our Redeemer.

Teaching that Christ had only one nature meant that Arius was among the first of the monophysites, which refers to those who held that Jesus had only a human nature and was raised to a kind of divinity — *mono* meaning "one" and *physis* meaning "nature." The Arian heresy was not a small localized movement: At one time almost all the bishops in the Eastern Church professed Arianism. St. Athanasius was one of the few who preserved the Orthodox faith in the Eastern Church, and his creed decisively defeated Arius's formulation. This heresy caused the emperor Constantine to call the first ecumenical council at Nicaea, which generated the Nicene Creed we say to this day at Sunday Mass. But Arianism outlived its founder and was a threat to the truth and unity of the Church for many generations.

A final point on Arius: He not only taught that the Word was created but that Jesus only assumed His *body* from the Blessed Virgin, and not a human soul. But this makes Christ akin to a monster. Every human man and woman has a human body, a human soul, a human will, and a human intellect. If Christ had no human soul, He couldn't have had a human intellect or will or emotions — only our bare flesh. Thus He could not have restored us by His perfect obedience because it wouldn't have been a human will that was obeying. In other words, this way of looking at Christ would compromise the atonement. Furthermore, this makes nonsense of the Jesus Christ described in the Scriptures, in which He expressed sorrow and anger and joy and surprise.

There were many other heresies that generated further councils to attempt to define Christological orthodoxy. To understand the definition the Church eventually canonized, it is important to note that the main terms in which revelation was defined come from Greek philosophy: nature, hypostasis, and person. "Nature," as the Church came to accept it, was a principle of action or movement. "Hypostasis," which we'll address more fully in the next chapter, meant an individual being exiting with a given nature. And "person" meant a hypostasis—an individual—with a reasoning nature, in other words a being with a human body and a human soul, with all that entails. The possession of a human soul implies having a human intellect, a will, passions, and a true physical body. The final definition of Christ given by the Church at Chalcedon, which we will examine further later on, was that in Jesus the union between humanity and divinity took place in His person, not within either nature, and that as a result each nature remained whole and entire as they acted in concert in the same individual, the same "hypostasis."

Every heresy that arose contributed to clarifying the final teaching—showing how God brings good out of bad. Apollinaris taught there was no human soul in Christ, that the Word took the place of the human soul. Obviously then, there could be no real human reactions in Jesus, and so He could not repair the damage done to the human race by the disobedience of Adam.

Euthyches was a monophysite who taught there was only one nature in Christ, which was both divine and human. Divine nature is perfect and infinite and cannot be changed. The only way it could combine with another nature is if it were changed, or the other nature changed into it, or both natures transformed into something that was neither human nor divine. This would not be human. But the Scriptures clearly teach that Jesus is a Son of David and a Son of Abraham.

Captivated by the Master

The Manichees thought that all flesh was evil, so they denied that Christ had a human nature and taught that His apparent flesh was spiritualized matter — in other words, that He had the body of a ghost, that He was human in appearance but not in reality. This not only would make Jesus a liar, but would make nonsense of His suffering and thus His atonement.

Related to this heresy is the teaching of Valentinus, who said that Christ had a real body, but it was created in heaven and so He took nothing from Mary: He passed through her body as water passes through a channel. Again, in this way of looking at things Mary would not be really Christ's mother. (This is why icons that portray the angel Gabriel bringing down the already incarnate child to Mary are heretical.) Christ received His body truly from her flesh, and His human soul was created in the Annunciation. He had to have this material connection with the race of Adam to redeem us from the sin of Adam.

We could go on and on. But rather than continuing to focus on Christological errors, let us now turn to the Christological truth that those heresies helped to uncover and define.

4

Christ in the Creeds

We say the Creed, usually the Nicene Creed, at every Mass. But how often do we actually examine the brilliantly complex and subtly explained truths in those few sentences? The Creed didn't come out of nowhere; it is the end result of decades of debate and is designed, in almost every word about Jesus Christ, to address major heresies that have circulated through history. Let's look at it line by line.

I believe in one Lord Jesus Christ, the Only Begotten Son of God, born of the Father before all ages.

You'll remember that some people, such as Arius and his followers, said that Christ was not a true son of God, and that He was not altogether divine. The very first words of the section of the Nicene Creed about Jesus address this error straightforwardly. We then affirm that Christ was born before all time to deny the heresy that He was created only in history.

God from God, Light from Light, true God from true God . . .

Now, some people accepted that Christ existed before He was conceived by the Blessed Virgin Mary, but they erred by saying that it was the *Father* Who was conceived or that Christ was the same Person as the Father. The formulation "God from God, Light from Light" shows that there is a distinction in persons but a unity in nature within the Trinity itself. The next phrase about Christ being the "true God" may seem redundant, but it addresses the error that accepts that Christ existed before the Blessed Virgin Mary and is different from the Father, but claims that He was Himself created. Thus we affirm that Christ and the Father both share one divine nature in its completeness.

. . . begotten, not made, consubstantial with the Father . . .

Another serious heresy, as we've said, was that Christ was something like a demigod: a very high creature, but still a creature. So we affirm that He was begotten but deny that He was "made," or created, by God. We then go on to say that He is "consubstantial" with God the Father in order to address the heresy that Christ was completely separate from and did not share a nature with the Father.

For us men and for our salvation he came down from heaven . . .

Here we turn to the errors that deny Christ's human nature. A famous theologian named Origen, for instance, thought that Christ was born to save even demons—that is, fallen angels. In order to hold this, though, Origen had to compromise the fact that the Lord took on *true flesh*. In this regard his thinking resembled another heresy called Docetism (related to Manichaeism from the last chapter), which taught that Jesus' flesh was only apparent. In response, the Creed affirms that Christ truly descended to us, and that He did so *for us*. This formulation also denies the adoptionist heresy of Photinus by asserting that Christ truly came from heaven: He was not a regular human being whom God simply adopted. In other words, He did not just go up to heaven but first came down from heaven.

. . . and by the Holy Spirit was incarnate of the Virgin Mary, and became man.

There were (and still are, of course) people, such as the Ebionites, who denied the virgin birth and claimed that Jesus was really the son of a human man and woman; thus the Creed says He was incarnate *by* the Holy Spirit and *of* the Virgin Mary. It's both; it's a divine-human cooperation. He did not just "pass through" Mary, as Valentinus claimed, but truly took His humanity from her. And He was, as we see in the last words of this sentence, fully human in body and soul. He was not only *apparently* human, not some kind of ghost. This was against Euthyches (neither God nor man), Arius and Appolinaris (no human soul), and Nestorius, who thought Jesus was in man as a man in a house but did not become man.

In 451, a century after Nicaea, the Council of Chalcedon further defined the orthodox faith by saying that Jesus is "one and the same Christ, Son, Lord, Only-begotten, to be acknowledged in two natures, without confusion, without change, without division, without separation." In other words, He is one Divine Person Who always existed in His divine nature, and at a certain point in time took upon Himself a human nature. The divine nature has always existed in God; the human nature began to exist in time in the Blessed Virgin. Therefore we can say that there are three substances in Christ, all united but not confused: the divine nature, the human nature, and the Divine Person. By "substance," we mean distinct and complete realities all marvelously united in Christ.

The union between God and Man can only take place in the Person of the Word. The concept "hypostasis" expresses this, hence the phrase "Hypostatic Union" to describe Christ. If the union took place *within the natures*, one of three illogical alternatives would follow. First the divine and human nature could both remain intact, but they would just be joined together like a pile of stones, or like two conjoined fingers that are detached from the hand. Without union in the person, the combination of the natures would be awkward, ineffectual, and temporary. This would tie into the adoptionist heresy, making Christ into a human being with a divine nature layered on top.

Second, the natures could be united but changed — the divine nature or the human nature transformed or adulterated into something different and less than what it was originally. But, first of all, God's divine nature cannot be changed: That would contradict the definition of divinity. God wouldn't be God if His nature could be changed or mixed together like chocolate and vanilla pudding. And if the human nature were changed, then Christ wouldn't have the same nature as His Mother, and thus would have no connection to Adam, compromising the atonement. Both natures have to be preserved intact.

The third alternative would be that the divine and human natures are not mixed or changed, but made imperfect. Christ's divine nature wouldn't be truly divine, and His human nature wouldn't be truly human. This alternative is also unacceptable because this would mean that Jesus is neither altogether God nor altogether man, compromising His redeeming mission from both sides. The natures must be preserved without division, without separation, and without confusion.

The union between God and man takes place, as we've said, *in the person of Christ.* God is not changed into flesh; rather, flesh is deified by union with the Person of the Word, while still remaining true flesh. This is what we call the hypostasis, which is defined as a being in a state of unity and integrity, a being that can stand in its own right. For example, a thought on its own would not be a hypostasis, nor would only the mind that does the thinking. But a *thinking man* who possesses a thinking mind and has a thought would be a hypostasis because he is complete, a whole principle, a stand-alone. A dog emotion or a dog tongue would not be a hypostasis, but the dog who possesses a dog emotion and a dog tongue would be. For human beings, being a hypostasis simply means being a person, being a unique and integrated center of activity.

For example, Peter does not differ from Paul because Peter has an intellect or a will or emotions or a body, or because Peter has eyebrows or ears or fingers. All those things have to do with our nature as human beings. Peter differs from Paul, in contrast, because he's a unique and unrepeatable center of action that possesses an intellect, a will, emotions, and a body, and acts with and through those powers. While there was no time before the existence of Christ's divine nature, there was a time before the hypostatic union. So when Christ says that before taking flesh He is God, we must understand that to be His Divine Person and His divine nature—this is the implication of the seven great "I Am" statements in St. John's Gospel. But after taking flesh, when Christ speaks of Himself in the first person, He *also* reflects the human powers that He has begun to assume in time.

Now, if we're talking about what is *one* and what is *multiple* in Christ, we can also say that everything that has to do with His nature comes in twos, beginning with the human and divine. For example, there are two births in Christ: the eternal birth of the Word in the Trinity and the birth in time in the womb of the Blessed Virgin. A more important duality is that of intellect and will, divine and human of each, which is essential for understanding the atonement, which we will discuss later on. There's a divine intelligence that the Lord as the Word shares with the Father and the Holy Spirit, and a divine will that the Trinity similarly shares. Then there's the human intelligence and the human will, which are like ours. What is one in Christ, however, is the Person, the unique Center Who acts uniquely using all of these powers, Who is capable of divine and human activity.

Traditional theology has called the acts of Christ that are simultaneous manifestations of divine and human activity the "theandric" acts. For example, there is the story of the woman who touched Christ's cloak, saying, "If I touch even his garments, I shall be made well." And Christ perceived "in himself that power had gone forth from him" (Mark 5:28, 30). So by virtue of His human nature the Lord could be touched by her and feel that touch, and by virtue of His divine nature He could heal her in that touch. In this one action He manifested His dual nature, the divine and human nature exercised by the same Divine Person. All of Christ's actions and sufferings were meritorious for us because the divine and human nature were joined together in the union of one center of action, one person.

This is very important when we apply certain terms to Christ: It's important to apply terms to His *unified person* and not confuse His distinct human and divine natures. So we can say that the Son of God is both eternal *and* born in time, but we can't say that His human nature is eternal nor that His divine nature was born in time. Similarly, we can say both that the Son of God is immortal and that He died. But we couldn't say, of course, that human nature is made divine by Christ's divinity. It doesn't work that way — though we can be *raised to* divinity through the merits of His life, Death, and Resurrection.

We have to be especially careful about extending these terms to the time before the Lord was incarnate. For example, it is true that Mary is the Mother of God the Divine Person when He became incarnate, but she is *not* the mother of His divine nature. Thus there are two Sonships in Christ (there's that duality again) as the Son of God and the son of Mary. We could say, though, that the son of Mary is eternal if by that we mean the Person of the Word, not merely His human nature. It's very important when using terms concerning Christ to recognize whether those terms truly express and apply to the truth of the unified Person or of His divine or human natures.

It is instructive here to present some of the Athanasian Creed, which addresses these matters with precision and conciseness.

1. Whosoever will be saved, before all things it is necessary that he hold the catholic faith; ...

20. So are we forbidden by the catholic religion to say; There are three Gods or three Lords.

21. The Father is made of none, neither created nor begotten.

22. The Son is of the Father alone; not made nor created, but begotten.

23. The Holy Spirit is of the Father and of the Son; neither made, nor created, nor begotten, but proceeding.

24. So there is one Father, not three Fathers; one Son, not three Sons; one Holy Spirit, not three Holy Spirits.

25. And in this Trinity none is afore or after another; none is greater or less than another.

26. But the whole three persons are coeternal, and coequal.

27. So that in all things, as aforesaid, the Unity in Trinity and the Trinity in Unity is to be worshipped.

28. He therefore that will be saved must thus think of the Trinity.

29. Furthermore it is necessary to everlasting salvation that he also believe rightly the incarnation of our Lord Jesus Christ.

30. For the right faith is that we believe and confess that our Lord Jesus Christ, the Son of God, is God and man.

31. God of the substance of the Father, begotten before the worlds; and man of substance of His mother, born in the world.

32. Perfect God and perfect man, of a reasonable soul and human flesh subsisting.

33. Equal to the Father as touching His Godhead, and inferior to the Father as touching His manhood.

34. Who, although He is God and man, yet He is not two, but one Christ.

35. One, not by conversion of the Godhead into flesh, but by taking of that manhood into God.
36. One altogether, not by confusion of substance, but by unity of person.
37. For as the reasonable soul and flesh is one man, so God and man is one Christ;
38. Who suffered for our salvation, descended into hell, rose again the third day from the dead;
39. He ascended into heaven, He sits on the right hand of the Father, God, Almighty;
40. From thence He shall come to judge the quick and the dead.
41. At whose coming all men shall rise again with their bodies;
42. And shall give account of their own works.
43. And they that have done good shall go into life everlasting and they that have done evil into everlasting fire.
44. This is the catholic faith, which except a man believe faithfully he cannot be saved.

The orthodox faith defines that there is one only begotten Son of God, and that He exists, will always exist, and has always existed with the Father in the Trinity. He gave up nothing of that eternal communion or of His divine nature in the Incarnation. His divine nature wasn't transformed into but was united with a human nature. That unity can never be reversed, and so Christ now maintains that human nature forever, thus opening for us the gates of heaven. It is necessary for us to affirm, then, that when we experience Christ's touch and see His eyes and hear His voice, we experience the Person of the Word. Let us believe and adore.

5

Full of Grace

And the Word became flesh and dwelt among us, full of grace and truth; we have beheld his glory, glory as of the only Son from the Father.... And from his fulness have we all received, grace upon grace. (John 1:14, 16)

What does it mean that Christ was "full of grace and truth"? This will be the theme of the next two chapters. Remember that Jesus has two natures and has thus two intellects and two wills, one of each divine and the other of each human. It goes without saying that Christ's divine nature has the fullness of grace and truth, so we will focus here on His human nature.

The idea that Christ was truly "full of grace" in His human nature is challenging for those who want to design a more "approachable" Jesus Christ. Some teach, for instance, that Christ experienced interior temptation and uncertainty, that He really lost the presence of God in the Garden and on the Cross. Some teach that Jesus didn't understand His calling and His destiny, that He was surprised by His Passion and Death. All of this, however, assumes that Christ was not in fact full of grace, that He lost full and confident communion with God the Father. And this is not possible.

The idea isn't new, however. There was the heresy of the Agnoetes, who believed that Christ was truly ignorant of His calling, and this was condemned by the Church. If Christ had lacked knowledge, then His divine nature would have been subsumed and overwhelmed by His human nature, and we know that can't have been the case because divinity is by definition unchanging and impossible to dilute. The self-emptying of Christ described in Scripture was not, and could not have been, the loss of His divinity.

Christ couldn't have experienced the lack of the presence of the Lord because that alienation is precisely the cause of the suffering and pain of original sin. All the other punishments—death, sickness, vacillation, malice, ignorance, and so on—are all just rotten fruits of that sin. Salvation according to Aquinas consists in the "enjoyment of God." How many of us can say we truly enjoy God? Sure, we call on Him when we're in trouble, and there's nothing wrong with that. But how many of us can say that at every moment we enjoy God interiorly as the focal point of our universe? Jesus Christ, full of grace and author of our salvation, has truly perfect enjoyment of God.

This enjoyment consists in two things: the satisfaction of the human will in love of God, and the satisfaction of the human intellect in knowledge of God. Human beings can only approach these perfections here on earth, but in heaven we can enjoy God in His fullness. Christ's human will and intellect, however, already and completely enjoyed this divine satisfaction. He adhered to God totally and spontaneously without any vacillation, enjoying Him in every moment. He *both* had complete communion with God *and* was a pilgrim on His way to God. John Paul II said in one of his conferences on theology of the body: "In his condition as pilgrim on the roads of earth, he was already in possession of the goal to which he would lead us" (May 4, 1980). But by an action of Christ's will, He kept the fullness of this grace and knowledge from arriving at His body—we'll talk about this in another program—so that He could suffer death for us.

What exactly is this grace with which Christ was blessed? At its most fundamental, grace is a true relationship between a person and God that effects a genuine change in the soul. Therefore grace is creative, bringing forth a new way of being. This is so much more than just God's external overlooking of sin, as some have claimed. It is rather a special help, wrought by the Holy Spirit, that brings about an interior change, making us truly pleasing to God. It is the elevation of man to Him so that we might know and love Him in His completeness. Through grace we become at peace with God.

The thing is that through all of this we still remain human persons, fallible and changeable. So we can always lose grace. Christ, on the other hand, at the instant of His conception as man, received the extraordinary grace for His holy humanity to be an instrument of His divinity. This perfection was instantaneous and eternal, impossible to be lost. Thus, He was always totally united with God.

The key is that Jesus is a true man, an integral man, and a perfect man. He is a true man because He has a human intellect, a human will, human passions, and a human body. He is an integral man because He has all of these in an ordered relationship that reflects how the soul and the body should naturally relate to each other. And He is a perfect man because He has the fullness of every experience of these powers. This last point will become important in the question of the human knowledge of Christ.

There are traditionally said to be three ways in which Christ enjoyed union with God through grace. The first is, simply, the grace of union, which we discussed in exploring the Hypostatic Union. This is the grace that made that wonderful and mysterious union possible. This is expressed in John 1:14 at the beginning of this chapter: "And the Word became flesh." This is a whole new way of speaking about the relationship of creation to God, and it is the source and the foundation of all the graces of Christ. No created being, including Mary, has ever experienced this grace.

The human nature of Christ is united to the person of the Word as a tool. Remember: This grace was not merited by Christ in His human nature; He didn't have to earn it. No, this is a grace by which human nature was elevated to the Divine Person so that the Divine Person could act through it. This miracle of miracles is unimaginable for us, that man could relate to God in His very person. But it is in His holy humanity as a tool of His divinity that God finally reveals the fullness of His nature.

The famous comparison is to the hand and the soul: The hand physically writes a novel but can only do so because it is connected to the reasoning soul. The human nature of Christ, including His spiritual human soul, is related to His divinity in a similar way: the means by which His divinity can act in the world. The soul is God's nature, which Jesus possesses as the person of the Word.

This grace of union is also the source of the theandric acts, which we have already examined. The flesh of Christ has the power to heal *in itself*. Even the clothing of Christ, externally connected to His body, takes on this power. The woman suffering from the hemorrhage merely touched the hem of His cloak and Jesus felt power going out from Him when she was healed (Mark 5:25–31). This intrinsic relationship between the bodily and the spiritual is reflected in the Church's sacramental theology, which holds that the sacraments are exterior, physical signs of interior, spiritual graces.

The second kind of grace is that given to Christ's human nature as a result of this union. This interior grace is the same sanctifying and actual grace that is offered to each of us by God the Father through the Spirit: the essence of the soul that elevates it to communion with God and stimulates the virtues and gifts that are the cornerstone of the spiritual life. Christ receives this, however, in a special and inalienable way, since by the grace of union He is the *natural* Son of God, not an adopted son. We all have to be elevated to God; Christ was conceived already in perfect union with Him, "full of grace and truth" (John 1:14). Through sanctifying grace, He experienced true union with the Trinity during His sojourn as man; and through actual grace God aided, supported, and protected Him. "When Christ came into the world, he said ... 'Lo, I have come to do thy will, O God'" (Heb. 10:5, 7). Thus God's love, the love that He expressed in taking on mortal human nature, is united to human love and human obedience so that Christ could satisfy for our sin.

We see this affirmed throughout Scripture. In Luke we read that Christ quoted Isaiah: "The Spirit of the Lord is upon me, because he has anointed me" (Luke 4:18, quoting Isa. 61:1). At Christ's baptism and Transfiguration, the Lord Himself speaks from heaven to tell the world, "This is my beloved Son" (at the Transfiguration He adds, "Listen to Him"; Matt. 3:17, 17:5; Mark 9:7). God the Father is speaking to us about His Son, Who, right there in front of us, was in His human nature one of us. Through this extraordinary grace He was the perfect instrument for divinity. A bent nail or a broken saw would be discarded by a carpenter as unfit for the task of constructing a worthy building; Christ's human nature was in no sense, and could never have been, unfit for the divine plan.

What about when Jesus went off to pray? Doesn't that suggest an imperfection in His union with the Father? The answer is no, because Christ didn't *have to* pray, at least in the way that we pray —haltingly, imperfectly, and so on. He was always at prayer in His very being. He went off to pray, therefore, to demonstrate the life of holiness for us, to give us an example to imitate. He taught us that to be a genuine minister of the Gospel we must go apart for a time. After raising Lazarus, Jesus said to His Father after praying, "I knew that thou hearest me always, but I have said this on account of the people standing by, that they may believe that thou didst send me" (John 11:42).

By this perpetual interior grace Christ merits no glory *of soul* for Himself, but rather the glory *of body* in His Resurrection, through His obedience in His Passion. But He merits for us the glory of *our souls and bodies* by elevating our nature. In this grace, the Lord Jesus possesses the complete and total fullness of all virtues and all gifts, both sanctifying and charismatic—and invites us to join Him. (The one virtue Jesus does not have is faith, because He already sees God perfectly and perpetually.) The charismatic graces such as healing and prophecy differ from sanctifying grace in that the charismatic graces exist not for personal sanctification, but for the salvation for others.

The third way Christ is "full of grace" is that He diffuses grace to others. By His obedient Death, everything Christ does becomes a means by which we share in the atonement—the remission of our sins and the reception of the gift of the Holy Spirit. This grace is called the capital grace, from the Latin word referring to the head. Christ is the head of the whole human race because through Him as our mediator and high priest, grace is transmitted to us. He is therefore also head of the Mystical Body of the Church. In Christ, this grace is in the essence and powers of His personal soul; in the Mystical Body of the Church, it is the communion of all the baptized in the state of grace. We receive the internal sanctification of the Holy Spirit through the external ministry of the Son because the Holy Spirit proceeds from both the Father and the Son. This is why the sacraments, as physical extension of the power of His body in heaven, are necessary to receive the Holy Spirit.

This capital grace flows naturally from the first two graces given to Christ: "from his fulness have we all received, grace upon grace" (John 1:16). All men, even those who are atheists, as long as they are alive on this earth are potentially members of His Mystical Body. The only people who are not even potentially members of this Mystical Body are those who cannot return to love of God: the damned in hell. All other human beings are either potentially members, in the sense that they're preparing themselves to join to Him, or members in either full or partial communion with Him.

The terms "head" and "members" of a body are used here only analogically. The difference between a mystical body and a physical body is this: a mystical body includes both those who are members right now and those who *could be* members, while a physical body is limited to the here and now, those who are actually members. We can also draw a distinction with a political body, which is united by goals and laws ordered toward peace and tranquility in this world. But in a mystical body, the goal is the final, spiritual fulfillment of human life, found in and through the infinite supernatural and uncreated power of the Holy Spirit. The union of the mystical body is not merely one in acting but, through baptism, one in being.

The unity of the Church is, by grace, the same unity that is found among the Father, Son, and Holy Spirit in heaven. Christ, in His human nature and His royal priesthood, makes this possible for us. After all, the Church is His Body, and He is in perpetual communion with the Trinity. A key text in Vatican II's Dogmatic Constitution on the Church, *Lumen Gentium*, is: "Thus, the Church has been seen as 'a people made one with the unity of the Father, the Son and the Holy Spirit'"[3] (no. 4).

The graces of Christ are threefold, expressing the unique union present in the human nature of Christ. His person is the Word, and the union of His nature in His person causes His humanity to be holy, with the fullness of the virtues in all His powers. He is head of His Body the Church, and so all our experiences of the grace and gifts of God have their source in His human nature.

---

[3] S. Cyprianus, *De Orat Dom.* 23: PL 4, 5S3, Hartel, III A, p. 28S. S. Augustinus, *Serm.* 71, 20, 33: PL 38, 463 s. S. Io. Damascenus, *Adv. Iconocl.* 12: PG 96, 1358 D.

6

Full of Truth

N ow let's turn to one of the most disputed questions of Christology in our time: Jesus' knowledge and consciousness. As
discussed in the last chapter, the Gospel of John tells us that Christ
was "full of grace and truth" (John 1:14). Elsewhere in Scripture,
however, we also read that Jesus "grew and became strong, filled
with wisdom; and the favor of God was upon him" (Luke 2:40).
And again: "Jesus increased in wisdom and in stature, and in favor
with God and man" (Luke 2:54). It's not hard to read into these
sentences that Christ was ignorant of Who He was. Some say that
the Lord didn't comprehend Who He really was until God's revelation at His baptism, or even until His Resurrection.

This has never been the teaching of the Church, however, and
skepticism of Christ's self-knowledge is in fact very recent. Thomas
Aquinas taught: "There is no perfection given to creatures which
may be withheld from Christ's soul which is the most excellent
of creatures."[4] The Catholic tradition has always held that Christ
assumed His nature and powers in His Incarnation as a means to
our redemption. Since to accomplish this redemption He assumed
an integral human nature as the head of the human race, He had
to assume something from every experience of human nature.

Human nature is found in three states: integrated nature before
the original sin; fallen and redeemed nature after the sin on earth;

[4] *Compendium of Theology*, 216.

and glorified nature after the resurrection of the dead. For Christ to truly assume the perfection of human nature, it was fitting for Him to participate in each of these states of nature in their relationship to God. Regarding His human intelligence, this means He had to assume infused knowledge from the state of original justice; experiential knowledge and abstraction from the state of original sin; and the beatific vision from the state of glorified nature in heaven.

Let's go into more detail about these states of human nature, and the qualities of knowledge proper to each. The state of Original Justice consists of what we call *condign* nature, which is our nature *as it ought to be*—that is, without sin. Adam enjoyed this state of nature when he was created in grace. What was characteristic of his experience that is not characteristic of ours, or even of the saints in heaven, is that Adam enjoyed *infused* knowledge. He experienced a continuous state of infused contemplation of God, including knowledge beyond what his senses could perceive—such as the natures of the animals he named. This is an important concept in Hebrew: to name something is to know its nature.

Regarding Christ, then, we cannot say that God the Father denied to Christ the knowledge He gave to Adam before the sin. We at least have to say that Christ had the knowledge of Adam. But we also have to go further: "Christ [is] the power and the wisdom of God" (1 Cor. 1:24). Thus we have to affirm that there is no perfection given to creatures—*including the perfection of heaven*—that was withheld from the soul of Christ.

He experienced this infused knowledge especially with regard to His mission. There are times when Jesus seems to deny this. Consider: "But of that day or that hour no one knows, not even the angels in heaven, nor the Son, but only the Father" (Mark 13:32). The *Catechism of the Catholic Church* addresses this problem: "By its union to the divine wisdom in the person of the Word incarnate, Christ enjoyed in his human knowledge the fullness of the divine plans he had come to reveal. That he admitted to knowing in the area, he elsewhere declared himself not sent to reveal" (474). In other words, it is not that Jesus as man *did not know this*, but rather it was not part of His mission to reveal it to us.

The second state of humanity is that of our fallen and redeemed nature: the Fall anticipates the redemption, and the redemption completes the Fall. What kind of knowledge is characteristic of this experience—*our* experience? Of course, when Adam sinned, ignorance entered the world. But that doesn't mean we aren't able to know anything at all. Rather, it means that man is limited to the kind of knowledge we can discover through our senses and experiences, from which we can extrapolate or abstract using our reason. This is the kind of knowledge that we all have now, the kind of knowledge that even the greatest philosophers have been limited to.

And the third state of human nature is glorified. None of us will be perfect until we see God in the Beatific Vision. "For now we see in a mirror dimly, but then face to face. Now I know in part; then I shall understand fully, even as I have been fully understood" (1 Cor. 13:12). The darkened glass is our limited perception here on earth; face to face we see and understand all. This knowledge of the vision of God is the highest knowledge any human being can have, and it's the completion of ourselves as spiritual beings. Nothing material or created can satisfy our desire for the infinite, our desire to know the causes of the world.

Because Christ's human soul—that is, His created soul—is the most excellent of created souls conceivable, He must enjoy the Beatific Vision on earth from the moment of His conception. If Christ did not, this would mean that the saints in heaven are greater than Christ was while He was on earth, and this is impossible. The saints in heaven, while they are now perfected, are still created human persons, not divine ones. Also, if Christ did not enjoy the Beatific Vision on earth it would have meant He was capable of sinning and would have had to merit divinity for Himself. We have to affirm, then, that the knowledge of Christ had to include, at the very least, everything human nature is capable of, in all its manifestations.

"Christ [is] the power and the wisdom of God" (1 Cor. 1:24). In Him we see every manifestation that human knowledge can take—beatific, infused, and acquired—all inscribed in one Divine Person with a human soul. Let's now turn to these three kinds of knowledge in more detail.

First, beatific knowledge is the experience of seeing God face to face, seeing all things through the Word in Whom God created the world. In Him were all things that were made, and without Him was made nothing that has been made. Through the Word, we experience and understand all of creation—every rock, plant, animal, and person—as He does. Christ, Who is the Word, then must experience this above all.

The question, as we've said, is whether He saw the vision of God from the moment of His conception. And the answer is: He absolutely must have. If Christ didn't experience the vision of God from the beginning, He would have been only a pilgrim on earth, just like us, fumbling around and trying to learn and improve. And He would have had to merit this improvement, this grace; thus He wouldn't have experienced the glory of soul that made Him the author of our salvation. In other words, He needed to possess heaven in all its wisdom and glory in order to give it to us. Christ, the natural son of God, must have possessed the Beatific Vision from the moment of His conception so that He could give it away to others.

This is because one who truly and securely has the vision of God can't experience even the possibility of committing sin. (This is why we affirm that Adam *did not* have beatific knowledge, but only infused knowledge, which he could betray.) Christ's soul on earth was more perfectly happy than the soul of any human being who ever lived. He experienced in His human soul the entire order of the universe; thus it is through Him that angels and men are both naturally enlightened as to the mysteries of creation.

But Christ's human nature did have limits. All of this was still happening within a human intellect, so He didn't experience the fullness of the world that He shared in the divine intellect with God the Father in the sense that in His human intellect, He didn't experience *all that it's possible for God to create.* Christ knew our creation through and through in His human intellect, but He didn't understand all possible creations, all possible arrangements of existence. Remember, though, that there are two intellects in Christ: He did have that perfect, comprehensive knowledge in His divine intellect.

The second kind of knowledge the Lord experienced was infused knowledge. This is characteristic more of the angels than it is of us. The angels receive inspiration and enlightenment from the light of God concerning the things that they are to know. We experience a similar enlightenment through prophetic vision, but Christ, because He was even more perfect, had an intuitive infused knowledge concerning all the things He experienced—beyond what His senses could perceive.

This wasn't some kind of magic—extrasensory perception or telepathy or something. It was real knowledge. Throughout the Gospels, we hear that Jesus knew the thoughts of those who intrigued against Him; this means that in His human intellect He experienced true knowledge that His senses could not immediately perceive. He perfectly understood the nature of everything in its relationship to God. He had this infused knowledge from the moment of His conception, which developed such that His obedience was always perfectly informed.

Some have said that, compared to this extraordinary knowledge, that of Christ's senses and human powers of abstraction must have been meaningless or unnecessary. But in Christ the senses and the intellectual knowledge they form were not vain, because they are the ordinary human means of knowing, and Christ was fully human. They were given to Him so that He might experience suffering and death in His body through His senses. This does not mean, however, that He had to be told what His mission was. He did not need to be taught by others that He was the Messiah or would have to suffer, die, and rise. No, by infused knowledge the Lord understood His mission, and He understood how the thoughts of men and the nature of everything in the world related to that mission.

This doesn't mean that the life of Christ was like a train on tracks, destined to only one route to only one destination without His human input or choice. His infused knowledge was, in fact, the source of His ability to make choices concerning His mission of redemption, allowing Him to examine each situation He encountered in its fullness. For example, during the agony in the Garden, He really did have to choose to embrace the Cross. What this means, though, is not that He had the option to choose against redemption, but that He had the option to choose different means to redemption. Of course, there was in fact only one way willed by the Father according to the order of justice and truth.

> The counsel of the Lord stands for ever,
> the thoughts of his heart to all generations.
> Behold, the eye of the Lord is on those who fear him,
> on those who hope in his steadfast love,
> that he may deliver their soul from death,
> and keep them alive in famine. (Ps. 33:11, 18–19)

Even Christ's thoughts are meant to rescue us from death. He is not only the Restorer but the Fountainhead of grace; His infused knowledge made Him perfectly able to understand the mysteries of grace and to pass them on to us.

And the third kind of knowledge in Christ is acquired or experimental knowledge. In ancient theology this was the most difficult knowledge of all to explain. Even the great St. Thomas had to correct himself, repudiating an earlier opinion that there was no acquired knowledge in Christ because it would have been superfluous given His beatific and infused knowledge. But, St. Thomas later understood, even this tremendous knowledge did not give Him a perfect experience of all the powers of man. This accords with the point that Jesus was not only true man and integral man but also perfect man. Had Christ not been able to experience ordinary experimental knowledge, which is characteristic of science and philosophy through reason, He would not have had the perfection of the use of the human intellect.

For example, Christ knew the nature of a rock from His communion with the Father, but in order to know how many pebbles were in a stream He would have had to count them. He would have known the nature of carpentry, but in order to learn the human craft He would have depended upon St. Joseph to show Him the details. Of course, He could have taught Himself, but He submitted to the lessons of His foster father in order to teach us to honor our parents and to show that the Incarnation wasn't meant to be frighteningly superhuman, but simply human. In experiencing a particular human being, Christ could even be surprised or amazed by that person's reactions or choices. For instance, with genuine and pleased surprise He told those around him, "Truly, I say to you, not even in Israel have I found such faith" (Matt. 8:10).

Some modern theologians who find the teaching that Jesus had beatific and infused knowledge contrary to His human nature suggest that it would have meant that He would have known, for instance, French before French developed. But this is not so. Jesus knew whatever aided His mission, and future languages would have undermined the witness of His humanity. The languages of His own time that aided His mission, on the other hand, He would have studied and understood. By "study" we don't mean in a book, but by experiencing them spoken by those around Him, including odd idioms and turns of phrase.

This is the only kind of knowledge in which Christ could have advanced: the particulars of everyday life perceived by the senses. This is what the Gospels mean when they say He advanced—not that He was ever ignorant or despairing, even on the Cross. Christ always enjoyed the Beatific Vision from the moment of His conception, otherwise He could not have merited salvation for us. He understood His mission to redeem the human race, and He understood how the natures of all things related to that mission and to God, because only by this knowledge could He perform meritorious acts for us.

John Paul II dwelt on this problem at length in his conferences on Christ. The following passage is long but quite direct and expresses this tradition well:

> To what extent was Jesus aware of this purpose of his mission (for us men and for our salvation): When and how did he perceive his vocation to offer himself in sacrifice for the sins of the world?... It is not easy to penetrate the historical evolution of Jesus' consciousness.... He was aware that over his head there hung that 'it is expedient' corresponding to the Father's original plan (cf. Mark 8:31) long before the historical circumstances were to lead to the fulfillment of what had been preordained.... In the Gospels we can find not a few other proofs of Jesus' awareness of his future destiny in accordance with the divine plan of salvation. Already when he was twelve years old, Jesus' reply on the occasion

when he was found in the Temple is the first expression in a certain way of this awareness.... Besides, it is evident from the Gospels that Jesus never accepted any thought or discourse that could hold our hope of earthly success of his work. The divine 'signs' he offered, the miracles he worked could provide a basis for such hopes. But Jesus did not hesitate to deny every intention, and to dissipate every illusion in that regard, because he knew that his messianic mission could not be fulfilled otherwise than through sacrifice.... We should note however, that in the texts quoted, when Jesus announces his Passion and Death, he speaks also of his Resurrection which takes place on 'the third day.' This does not in any way affect the essential significance of the messianic sacrifice by death or the Cross, but on the contrary, it emphasizes its salvific and life-giving meaning. This pertains to the most profound essence of Christ's mission: the World's Redeemer is he in whom is fulfilled the Pasch, that is, the passage to a new life in God.[5]

Thus the Lord Jesus Christ, by His perfect knowledge, was able to see how all the things in the world fit into the plan of God. He was conscious both of Who He was and of what His mission was. His atoning work demanded that He know what was happening to Him, and that from moment to moment He embrace this destiny by a human choice filled with God. Only in this way could He truly atone for our sin and disobedience. We need only look to the words of Christ Himself for confirmation: "No one takes it from me, but I lay it down of my own accord. I have power to lay it down, and I have power to take it again; this charge I have received from my Father" (John 10:18).

---

[5] Wednesday audience discourse, October 5, 1988.

7

Jesus the "Imperfect"?

W e've talked a lot about Christ's perfection; now let's consider His apparent weaknesses. Taking on human nature meant that Christ took on real limitations. Understanding the precise nature of those limitations is essential to understanding Christ's saving mission. St. Thomas Aquinas used the term "defects" for these limitations, but this shouldn't be taken to mean genuine faults, but rather aspects of Christ that seem to run counter to His divinity, such as His ability to suffer and to die.

In contemporary theology, though, some have expanded these to include the ability to sin, concupiscence or weakness of the passions, and even ignorance and vacillating in doing the will of God. We've discussed ignorance before, and will discuss vacillation later, so here we'll focus on pain, suffering, and the experience of the passions—especially the moral weakness of concupiscence, which is the bent of the passions toward sin.

There are some Scripture verses that have tripped people up in this regard. In the Letter to the Hebrews, for instance, we read: "For because he himself has suffered and been tempted, he is able to help those who are tempted" (Heb. 2:18). In Romans, St. Paul writes that God sent "his own Son in the likeness of sinful flesh and for sin" (Rom. 8:3). Some have read these as affirmations that Christ experienced internal temptation, that He at least *fantasized* about sin. But, as we have emphasized time and again, everything Christ assumed in the Incarnation was assumed for love of us and for our redemption — the perfection of wisdom and power and grace, all of which are the goals of human nature. But temptation is not one of those goals; it's not, as we will discuss, "more human" to be tempted to sin. Christ assumed the conditions of human nature that were necessary *to free us* from sin.

We've already analyzed the original sin from several points of view, but here let us say that, as with all evil, it involves a lack in being and a lack in acting. In physical evil — that is, defects of our physical nature — the lack in being causes a lack in acting: my lame leg makes me unable to walk perfectly. But when it comes to moral evil, a lack in acting causes a lack in being. My will, through my own fault, loves a temporal good in a disordered way, and this causes me to perform an act to attain this temporal good, be it wealth or pleasure or power, that brings disorder to my soul and the loss of sanctifying grace. In failing to act for the highest good, my soul has truly become *less* than it was. In this state, I cannot go to heaven.

The evil of acting, or evil of fault, causes the evil of being — punishment — which occurs in response to the disordered act. In Jesus, though, there can be no evil of fault. Yet He had to embrace some punishment — some evil of being — to atone for our sins. He could not embrace ignorance, malice, or concupiscence because these would compromise His perfect loving obedience.

Some think this makes Him "less approachable" as a human being, but this gets it all wrong: Sin and moral weakness don't make someone *more* human, but *less* human. If we find Him "more relatable" as a sinner, *that is an example of our fallen nature*, and should not be celebrated.

After all, the most fitting way of vicariously satisfying the demands of justice is to take on someone else's punishment, to pay someone else's penalty in its fullness. In Original Sin, by our fault we were diverted from God, thus we experienced punishment in our ability to see and experience Him, and in the frailty of our bodies—that is, moral and physical suffering. We aggravate this condition personally through our personal sins. Christ, lacking our moral imperfections but sharing our physical ones, could accept punishment in our place, thus satisfying the order of justice. He did this because He loves us. He experienced suffering and death especially on the Cross in atonement. "[He] emptied himself, taking the form of a servant ... he humbled himself and became obedient unto death, even death on a cross" (Phil. 2: 7–8).

Remember that this satisfaction required perfect obedience to satisfy for our disobedience. No single human being could do this because we had committed injustice against God Himself—an infinite crime. And the principal punishments for that sin, that is from the original sin and down through history, are suffering and death—an infinite punishment. And so a person of infinite goodness needed to take on—and then subvert—this infinite suffering.

What does this mean for the moral punishments resulting from original sin, such as vacillation and temptation? Christ could not have experienced those because they would have impeded the necessary perfect obedience. But He could, and had to, take on the physical, temporal penalty of suffering and death. It was not fitting for Christ to assume any defects in His Incarnation that would have detracted from His mission to satisfy for our disobedience. It was not fitting, that is, for Him ever to be separated from God by the loss of grace, by ignorance, by the loss of virtue, by concupiscence, or by any moral disorder. This does not make Christ less human, but perfectly human, as we were made to be.

The only punishments Christ could have assumed, then, were those physical limitations that pertain to our shared human nature: hunger, thirst, pain, mortality. These are the general sufferings of the human race. It would not have been fitting, on the other hand, for Him to assume any strictly individual imperfections or disorders, such as the flu or blindness. These general sufferings, though, are assumed because Jesus took flesh from the race of Adam. Had Christ's body been born from the dust of the earth as was Adam's, He would not have inherited any part of the original sin. Christ and Mary have these things only as a result of their material nature, not as a result of sin. Since Christ's body was formed by the Holy Spirit, though, and not by the power of human seed, His connection with Adam was only through the sinless flesh He took from Mary.

Thus we can say that Christ has no defect of body or soul. His soul is full of grace and truth. His body is perfectly formed by the Holy Spirit. Whatever He did or suffered with that body and soul was for our perfection. So He hid His divinity to make His humanity clearer, and He suffered death because of the necessity of nature and not because He had to for any moral reason. He had no sin, either actual or original, and also no weakness of the passions (concupiscence); His obedience even in the face of death was always voluntary.

But Christ's control of His passions didn't mean He was insensitive or unfeeling, in body or spirit. Quite the opposite: The Lord, fashioned by the power of the Holy Spirit, was the most sensitive human being Who ever lived. He *felt* more acutely than any of us do — including the feeling of pain because His body was most perfectly human. When He was cut, He suffered greater pain than we do. But He also felt purer pleasure: He naturally desired and enjoyed all those things that are reasonable to enjoy. He savored food and drink and sleep — but He did so in a different way than we do.

Every passion, every feeling, and every emotion in Christ was subservient to reason. His anger, for instance, was never out of control, but always perfectly calibrated to the offense. In our fallen nature, anger can build and burst in us before we can apply reason to it, but for Christ this could not happen. Some say that Jesus "lost his temper" in the Temple when He chased out the money changers, but great anger does not have to mean a loss of control.

Christ's anger was always tailored to the situation. When He wept, it was from fitting sorrow. When He rejoiced, it was over something truly good.

While Christ never experienced interior temptation to sin, He certainly understood the difference between a sin and a virtuous act. So we must affirm that He *chose* goodness and obedience. Thus when St. Paul says that Jesus was sent "for sin," (Rom. 8:3, above) it doesn't mean that He was sent *in order to sin* but *because of our sin.* Christ was a victim of sin, the most sensitive of human beings, Who showed us what our disobedience, our rejection of God's grace, does to the human person—even the best possible human person. We can see, then, the relationship between the tree in the Garden of Eden and the tree of the Cross on Calvary: the pleasurable catalyst of the first sin, and the painful instrument of its atonement.

Despite His extraordinary sensitivity, Christ could never seek any illicit or selfish goal in His pain or pleasure. He enjoyed and suffered always with our good in mind. When He fasted in the desert for forty days and nights, He genuinely got hungry, yet He did not endure this for His own perfection or satisfaction but as an example to us. When Jesus rejected Satan's temptation, it wasn't because He wasn't hungry, but because He had the perfect integrity of the will—the perfected human will—to be able to choose to obey the law of God even in the face of His great hunger.

We can learn a lot about the spiritual life from the way Christ experienced emotions—incredibly strongly, but always reasonably. It's a reminder that feelings are human: We aren't meant to be androids or Vulcans, the *Star Trek* aliens who suppressed all emotions in favor of "pure" logic. Our feelings don't have to lead us astray; it is possible—essential—to feel strongly and to choose well. Christ had, therefore, what theologians call "pro-passions," which are perfectly ordered passions that emerge from the proper judgment of the intellect and will. They may be negative and strong, but they were always ordered from and to truth and goodness. The agony in the Garden was so intense that Jesus sweat blood: "My soul is very sorrowful, even to death" (Matt. 26:38). But this was not despair. When Christ wept over Lazarus, it was because of the genuine pain of death and loss. It was also for our instruction.

There have been many erroneous theories of emotions through the ages. The Stoics believed that the emotions were sicknesses of the soul. Now, if we let our reason become subservient to our emotions, then this isn't far from the truth — but it doesn't have to be that way. Emotions are not *necessarily* disordered; they have an essential place in our souls. We feel sorrow, for instance, because there are things that are genuinely sorrowful. And so did Christ, and it was good and reasonable that He do so. Buddhism teaches that we overcome illicit desires by destroying the desires themselves by transcending their personal experiences and their very identities and entering into some kind of universal force. Since suffering is something that only individuals experience, the theory goes, the only escape is to deny our individuality by entering an alternate state of consciousness. Thinking and will are not a part of this experience; in fact, they are thought to be barriers to it. And since God is impersonal, there is no need for redemption, no need to order our personal powers, only to leave them behind. On the opposite end of the spectrum, the prevailing notion today is that all feelings and desires are worthy, and that to try to apply reason to them is dangerous. However, it is this denial of reason, not exerting control over the passions, that is truly inhuman.

Christ shows how all these ways of thinking about emotions fall short; He demonstrates how feelings and truth must be related. In Christ there was no interior temptation with respect to the emotions because they were under the control of His reason, which means they were tethered to truth. Our willingness to follow our emotions *against* our reason is one of those moral punishments that could not have afflicted Christ without detracting from His salvific mission. Christ also took flesh to redeem us by His example. If He had been vacillating or morose or despairing, it not only would have distracted Him from the will of God but it would have damaged the perfect example He made for us.

These truths are aptly demonstrated in Christ's temptation at the beginning of His public ministry when, as the new Adam, He went into the desert to be confronted by Satan. The devil tempted Christ with three apparent goods, each of which could involve disordered passions: food for the body, vainglory in tempting God, and the pride of life. Jesus could have dismissed Satan, but instead He submitted to temptation for our instruction. He wanted to teach us that no one in this life, no matter how holy, is free of temptation: After baptism we still suffer from disordered passions that war against the life of grace. To strengthen us in our daily struggle with those passions, Jesus overcomes Satan not with a flourish of divine power but with the sheer goodness of a human will filled with divine grace. To persevere in grace when tempted, we must rely on Him.

Christ teaches us that we don't escape our feelings of sorrow and pain by destroying them. These natural weaknesses don't have to be moral weaknesses. Indeed, we could say the virtue of any true and good person is proved in how one handles the feelings, positive and negative, including especially suffering, that every person experiences throughout life. Christ certainly suffered intense sorrow due to the evils perpetrated against Him — the physical pain, yes, but perhaps more so the pain of betrayal. Jesus wept, too: He wept over the death of His friend Lazarus, and He wept over Jerusalem. But Christ's sorrow never degenerated into despair. Rather, His sadness was always tied to true goods — and of course it never led Him to disobey God.

Christ experienced, that is, the best and purest forms of human passions. The human soul at peace with God and itself doesn't lack feelings or destroy them, but rather cherishes them in their proper place: subservient to reason, ordered toward the true and the good. This is true integrity.

Whatever defects Christ assumed, He did so not because He needed to be redeemed or because He was obligated, but because He loved us. Everything about Him—including His defects—is ordered to our redemption.

8

He Wills It

In order for Christ to atone for our sin, it was necessary that He exercise true acts of human obedience in our place. This means, though, that His human will had to have a certain autonomy within His Divine Person: Otherwise, Christ the man would have been merely a puppet of Christ the divine. There has to be a true and real distinction between the divine will in Christ and the human will in Christ because it is the human will in Christ that truly merits, that truly satisfies for our sin. How could Christ reverse the unloving disobedience of Adam in His human will if He did not have a human will Himself? Indeed, as the second Person of the Holy Trinity, Christ the Word shares one divine will with the Father and the Holy Spirit. But this cannot replace or overwhelm His human will if He is truly to atone for our sin.

What does Christ's *human will* merit for Himself? We know, of course, that Christ's soul possessed the Beatific Vision from the moment of conception, so there is nothing more that His soul could merit. But Christ's *body* is a different matter. Christ, by His obedience, merited His bodily Resurrection, for us. He chose to take on those punishments for our sin that we share, but that do not affect the freedom of the will: suffering and death.

It was essential, then, that Christ's understanding and love *as God* could not replace His understanding and love *as man*; otherwise He could not stand in our place. He had to be autonomous in His human will; that is, His human nature had to be a distinct locus of action within Him. Jesus could not have been a marionette subjected to divine manipulation. Rather, He had to cooperate freely in the elevation of His soul, whether as a carpenter in the shop of St. Joseph or dying on the Cross for us, in order to merit glory in His humanity that would be applied to all of humanity. The Lord's human nature is an instrument of His divinity, and God never acts against our nature, which is to be free. Thus, in order for Christ to be our high priest and our mediator it was absolutely necessary for Him to be free in His choices.

None of Christ's perfections or sources of divine knowledge compromised His human freedom. In fact, they assured that Christ's free actions perfectly served God and that everything that He did was a means for our salvation. This may seem contradictory — and it has led some people and groups into heresy in ages past. This issue was of particular concern at the Third Council of Constantinople in the seventh century, where two heresies were condemned: monoenergism and monothelitism. Monoenergism, which clearly includes the root of "energy," held that there was a single "energy," a single means or place of activity in Christ, rather than dual human and divine ones. Monothelitism, on the other hand, asserted that there was only one kind of action, only one will in Christ.

These heresies are extensions of monophysitism, which held that there is only one nature in Christ. The people who affirmed this notion denied the theandric acts that we have discussed, asserting that they represented one action of one will and one nature. But, as we have discussed, this is impossible: The ability of Christ to touch in a human way comes from His human nature, but the power to heal with that touch comes from His divine nature. Christ is one person Who acted in two ways.

The Third Council of Constantinople definitively stated that in Christ "each nature wills and performs the things that are proper to it in a communion with the other." Thus the divine nature acted in ways proper to divinity and the human nature in ways proper to humanity, yet they are not separate but share a perfect unity in Christ's Person. The Council concluded: "We hold that two natural wills and principles of action meet in correspondence for the salvation of the human race." In Christ, therefore, there is a perfect communion between God and man. As there is a perfect communion in *being*, there is also a perfect communion in *action*. This communion requires distinction: one cannot be in communion with oneself, but there must be something *other*.

We can see this in the fact that Christ had to exercise choice in everything He did (His humanity), and yet He could not sin (His divinity). He chose among various good means to the good end of redemption. But He could not choose evil means. Indeed, to choose evil is not a sign of the fullness of humanity, but a defect of both humanity and freedom. When Jesus speaks in the first person, He does so as a single Divine Person, but with two different centers of action that are always in communion with each other.

The Fathers at Constantinople reflected on a marvelous summary of Catholic doctrine on this matter made by Pope Leo I in a letter to Flavian of Constantinople. This letter had already been used to arrive at the definition of the Council of Chalcedon. Now it underscored the issue of the autonomy of Christ in obeying the Father as man:

> The character of each nature, therefore, being preserved and unity in one person, humility was assumed by majesty, weakness by strength, mortality by eternity […] Each nature does what is proper to each in communion with the other: The Word does what pertains to the Word and flesh what pertains to the flesh. One shines forth in miracles, the other succumbs to injuries. And just as the Word does not depart

from equality with the Father's glory, just so the flesh does not abandon the nature of our race. (DS 293, 295)

We can see this human freedom coupled with divine mission in Scripture. Jesus says in John's Gospel: "For this reason the Father loves me, because I lay down my life, that I may take it again. No one takes it from me, but I lay it down of my own accord. I have power to lay it down, and I have power to take it again; this charge I have received from my Father" (John 10:17–18). In Hebrews we read, "Consequently, when Christ came into the world, he said, '... Lo, I have come to do thy will, O God'" (Heb. 10:5, 7). Elsewhere, Christ talks very specifically about His will and the will of God the Father, first in the Bread of Life discourse and second in the Garden of Gethsemane: "For I have come down from heaven, not to do my own will, but the will of him who sent me" (John 6:38); "not as I will, but as thou wilt" (Matt. 26:39). This raises the questions: How could the Lord have freedom of choice and yet be unable to sin? Could He have been drawn in His human will not to do the will of God?

As human beings we have conflicts within us, as our wills are drawn to various levels of good. Suppose I know that tomorrow I am going to have my gangrenous hand amputated without anesthetic, or else it will kill me. Since my will has various levels because my being has various levels, I can look on this surgery as either desirable or undesirable. For example, I can desire it from the point of view of saving my life, and I can find it undesirable because of the sensible pain that it will cause. So the will at a lower level—the level of sense—can find repugnant something that the will at a higher level—the level of survival—can understand to be good.

Let's take a less extreme example. I can love food as good because of its taste, or because it provides me with the sustenance needed to thrive. From another point of view, however, I can look at denying myself food as being *spiritually* good, such as in fasting, or saving money on luxurious meals in order to be able to give to the poor. Thus two seemingly opposite options can each be desirable at different levels of the will, and so we don't have to "override" our wills, or be coerced, to choose either. For instance, during fasting I can find hunger difficult on only the level of my senses while I find fasting enjoyable on the level of my intellect, on the level of the universal things. My accepting of the discomfort of hunger is a legitimate act of my will, not a violation of its freedom.

Thus the sensible aspect of Christ's human will might truly have found some suffering repellant, but He could still truly embrace it and freely choose it because His human will *also* recognized the higher goodness of higher things—that is, our salvation. So on one level Christ's feelings could really shrink from doing the will of God, since He understood that the will of God would cause Him suffering and He truly felt sorrow and fear at such suffering. He didn't deny or destroy these feelings because what He faced was *truly* fearful and sorrowful. Yet on a higher level He could still choose this path completely and without vacillation because of the greater good involved.

Christ had full freedom of choice and freedom from sin because at the same time He experienced the vision of God that is the end of His pilgrimage and He was still a pilgrim here. In other words, He looked at everything in this life from the point of view of its destiny, already realized. Further, Aquinas maintains that there must be knowledge that the evil about to be suffered will not last forever in order to sustain hope. Therefore Christ could not have freely chosen suffering in His agony in the Garden unless He already knew that He would rise from the dead.

To say that freedom of choice and the inability to sin are incompatible would also be to say that the saints who now enjoy the vision of God make no choices. But the saints choose all the time, for instance in interceding for people who pray to them. They don't have to choose in the same sense that Christ did, in the face of pain and emotional sorrow, fear and despair, but they retain the free will that is essential to human nature, which is not destroyed in perfection. Christ was like this: He looked at the world from the top down, from the point of view of the fullness of human life already realized. He regarded time from the point of view of eternity. He did not have to ask why anything was happening.

Some say that Christ's anchor in heaven means that He couldn't have experienced the same pain we do. Remember, though, that His humanity—body and emotions and so on—was extraordinarily sensitive because He was generated in true flesh in the womb of Our Lady by and through the Holy Spirit. So Christ suffered more than we would, not just because of the sensitivity of His body but because, having already arrived at the vision of heaven, He could truly appreciate the horror of our sin and the rejection of God more than anyone else who has ever lived. His passions were perfectly formed, which means He would have felt more acute sorrow, fear, and anxiety than we do.

Christ had a free will confirmed in grace that allowed Him to choose the means of obedience, even if not the ends, and this did not give any less merit or autonomy to His obedience. The rest of us all vacillate in our choices because we haven't yet arrived at the vision of God, and so we don't yet fully comprehend how God is our happiness. Thus we don't have as deep a suffering from or revulsion at sin as Christ did. Our choices are characterized by hesitation and searching for meaning. We can fool ourselves about sin; He could not. So in Christ's choice there is no imperfection, but also no searching and no hesitation, which in us are the result of the loss of grace.

This is why Christ could fear the Cross at the same time that He chose it, knowing full well the horrors He was atoning for, and thus the good He was doing. He did not embrace this suffering *as suffering*—He was not a masochist—but He did so reasonably, fully, and freely as a just and redeeming act from the point of view of His higher self. It was a fit means by which we might be given back the glory of our souls and the glory of our bodies. "Although he was a Son, he learned obedience through what he suffered" (Heb. 5:8). "Learning" here does not mean He was ignorant of His identity. To learn in the sense of the Hebrew word means to experience. So He carried out His obedience in the freely chosen acts of His Passion.

For a person who truly understands the final picture and purpose of life, obedience in the face of physical torment is not a limitation of the human will, but its perfection, allowing the will to choose what is truly best in view of heaven and earth—in view of God. Christ could freely choose to give up His bodily life because He knew about the Resurrection, because He knew that, for God, death never has the final word. In these acts of will Christ does not show us a puppet manipulated by God, but a fully human nature that is *both* a tool of divinity *and* genuinely autonomous. Christ, in the face of suffering, truly and freely chose to redeem us.

9

The Early Years

In the first part of this book, the subject has been Christ's identity. Now let's turn more specifically to His life, which is traditionally considered in four parts: His entry into the world, His way of life in the world; His passage from the world, and His exaltation in the next world. The next chapters will treat each of these in succession.

Starting at the very beginning: The first proclamation of the gospel takes place in Genesis 3:15, when the Lord says to Satan, "I will put enmity between you and the woman, and between your seed and her seed." Here we are informed that the final enemy of Satan, the Messiah, will be born of a woman. This, in the fullness of time, is His entry into the world. Mary had to be made a fit receptacle for the miracle of the Incarnation; thus she had to be holy and pure, a virgin both spiritually and physically.

There are three actors in the drama in the Garden: the woman, the child, and the serpent. The same three actors then close the drama in Revelation 12: the woman, the child, and the dragon — a serpent who is greater, more dangerous, and more frightening. Eve, the first woman, submitted to the serpent in unloving disobedience and her fruit was sin. The new woman must therefore be without any sin, either personal or Original, so she can begin the redemption by lovingly obeying in place of Eve. And so by a special privilege she could and did avoid all sin in her life, demonstrating the powerful action of grace in her.

Captivated by the Master

Mary is the true Theotokos, the mother of God. In her, God the person of the Word took upon Himself a new relation, the relation of man to God *in person*. Nothing internal about God changed in the Incarnation, of course: *His* nature did not and cannot change. But man's relationship to God does change; in Mary, a new way of existing in relationship with God becomes incarnated. Nature is now related to God in His very Person.

Before the sin, the order between men and women was that of a wise governor to a free citizen — not, as some revisionists say, that of a master to a slave. The submission of women was one of the evils that resulted from the original sin. She seeks to dominate man by guile; he, by power. "Your desire shall be for your husband, and he shall rule over you" (Gen. 3:16).

The fact that men and women are meant to be genuine cooperators is shown when God creates woman not from the head of man (in which case she would be his superior), nor from his foot (in which case she would be his inferior), but rather from his side. In the redemption, therefore, woman must take part, just as she took part in the first sin, to show her full participation in the human race. Redemption, then, begins with woman and her obedience just as the Fall began with woman and her disobedience. And redemption is completed in Christ's obedience just as the Fall was completed in Adam's disobedience.

So Mary reverses the wicked Eve's Annunciation — that is, Eve's discourse with Satan, a fallen angel, which tempted her to eat of the fruit of the forbidden tree and thus to disobey God. In Mary's Annunciation, on the other hand, the Blessed Mother was asked to obey the Lord and to partake of a fruit, in this case the fruit of her womb, Jesus. And the Blessed Virgin was specifically prepared to receive the Annunciation of the good angel by the Immaculate Conception, which freed her from the least taint of original sin. In her life, Mary suffered neither from moral weakness nor from the physical effects of Original Sin. She had no pain in childbearing, and if she did suffer a kind of death, it was not a painful or corrupting one. She did suffer intensely, but her suffering was all connected with the human suffering of her Son. "A sword will pierce through your own soul" (Luke 2:35). She didn't experience suffering *as a punishment*, but rather as simply natural to humanity, in the same way as Christ.

Let's look at how God prepared Mary at the Annunciation. The angel Gabriel is like the minister who reads the vows for the marriage between heaven and earth in the person of the Blessed Virgin. He comes before her and bows and greets this young girl, and in so doing he changes the course of all the rest of human history. When angels came before men in the Old Testament, it was the custom for men to bow before them and say "hail." Here, though, the angel bows before a woman and says "hail." The grace Mary received is even greater than the angels; she surpasses them in her association with God and in her dignity.

Next the angel gives her a new title, "full of grace." Mary is truly full of grace because she was sanctified at the instant she received her soul, which prepared her throughout her life for marriage to the Trinity. Mary's perpetual virginity was essential to this nuptial relationship because she had to be completely available to the Trinity in her association of divine grace. Her union with the Trinity was unimaginably profound: God the Father was the father of her child; God the Holy Spirit was the means by which her child was generated in the womb; and God the Son, the Word made flesh, lived in her womb. When she is told she is to be the mother of the Messiah, she questions not because she doubts but because she wants more knowledge so her consent can be more complete. "How can this be, since I have no husband?" (Luke 1:34). Gabriel's reply invokes the entire Trinity, Holy Spirit then Father then Son: "The Holy Spirit will come upon you, and the power of the Most High will overshadow you; therefore the child to be born will be called holy, the Son of God" (Luke 1:35).

Gabriel's discourse with Mary—his reading of the marriage vows between her, as representative of mankind, and the Lord—fulfills three purposes. First, in allowing Mary to conceive first by faith—in her mind before her body—Eve's mental-then-physical disobedience is recalled and reversed. Second, this is as an image of our own conception of Christ, our own coming to understand and love Him: it begins with catechesis, with being told about Him. Third, through His messenger God calls forth from Mary the gift of her own obedience, again recalling and reversing Eve's wickedness. Importantly, this does not deny Providence in her; it was by this Providence, the fullness of grace in her, that God willed her consent.

Turning to the conception of Christ, we can begin by observing that, as with so much in Him, it was twofold: the human contribution of Mary and the divine, miraculous contribution of the Holy Spirit. The Holy Spirit was the agent by which Christ's flesh was generated in Mary's womb. Christ was not first conceived as man, and then later on assumed into the person of the Word: This leads to heresies such as adoptionism. There was no preexisting human person Who then became divine; there was rather a preexisting Divine Person Who, by the agency of the Holy Spirit, became human, taking on Himself a human body and a human soul as a human tool of His divinity.

Sanctifying grace in Christ is derived from this grace of His union in the womb of Mary. In all other human beings, the lesser perfection precedes the greater. "The first man Adam became a living being; the last Adam became a life-giving spirit" (1 Cor. 15:45). In Christ's case, though, the first perfection led to all His other perfections. The descent of the divine to the human in Christ is more important than the ascent of the human to the divine. There is no growth of grace in Christ because in Christ we find the fullness of grace present from the moment of His conception. There is no movement from sin to justification. There is rather a movement from simple divinity to divinity fused to humanity, instantaneously.

Christ from the moment He came into the world was both sanctified and, in His holy humanity, sanctifying. That is, He was sanctified in the womb so that He might sanctify us. Christ's coming into the world included not only His Incarnation, which we celebrate as the Annunciation, but to His becoming known to the world, which we celebrate at Christmas and Epiphany. Thus from the very beginning of His earthly life He sanctified not just by His presence, but by His example.

The first proclamation of this mystery occurred when Mary visited her cousin Elizabeth. She is the Ark of the Covenant carrying Jesus in her womb, and she is motivated by practical charity to care for her cousin, an old woman who is pregnant. Elizabeth echoes the man in the Old Testament who took the Ark into his house when it was deemed too dangerous to bring into Jerusalem: "And why is this granted me, that the mother of my Lord should come to me?" (Luke 1:43). Mary then evangelizes Elizabeth with the spectacular Magnificat: "My soul magnifies the Lord" (Luke 1:46). She is the first preacher of the gospel.

Let's now turn to His birth—especially to those who are the first to be informed of the Incarnation of the Son of God. It's not kings or priests or other leaders, but the shepherds—the ordinary unlettered men of the countryside. Not only are they informed, but they are granted the grace of an angelic visitation—the same beings who announced the covenant in the Old Law. We see here, first of all, a foreshadowing of Christ's identity as the Good Shepherd, but also the initial sign that He is coming with good news for all—especially the poor and ordinary. The shepherds also represent the announcement to the Jews of His entry into the world.

The second people who experience Christ's divinity in holy humanity are the Magi — noble philosophers, from beyond Israel. Whereas the Jewish shepherds received an angelic announcement, these educated Gentiles receive the news of Christ from the Star, thus through their senses and the application of their reason. They represent the entry of Christ into the world being made known through science and philosophy. It is nature (the star) which leads them to Christ. In response they bring gifts of faith: gold representing Christ's kingship, frankincense representing His divinity, and myrrh representing His suffering.

There is another important man, though, who violently rejects the good news: Herod, ruler of the Jews who out of jealousy despises holy humanity and holy wisdom. He should be the first to accept, but instead he rejects. The Magi, on the other hand, are pagan philosophers, but they identify Christ with holy wisdom, the One Who will resolve their wonder at the causes of the world. Since salvation comes from the Jews, the star leads them first to Jerusalem to consult the Hebrew Scriptures and then on to Bethlehem.

Then, Christ is circumcised and receives His name. The rite of circumcision was essential to becoming sanctified as a member of the community of Israel. Now, Christ did not have to submit to this because He didn't need to be sanctified, but He did so anyway for several reasons. First, the cutting itself showed the truth of His flesh. Second, He wanted to show His submission to a rite that had been commanded by God. Third, He wanted to show that He was from the clan of Abraham, since the Promised One was to come from Abraham. Fourth, He wanted to give no scandal to the Jews, in turn teaching obedience to the laws of the Covenant. Finally and most fittingly of all, Christ's circumcision was a prelude to His Passion, the first shedding of His blood by which He accepted the burden of the law upon Himself. The conferral of His name is the first time the Holy Name of Jesus is spoken in history, and it is Joseph who does so at the command of the angel.

The role of Joseph is also central to the entry of Christ into the world so that the Son of God can be perceived by the world as a normal man, raised and taught by a human mother and father. Some scriptural translations present Joseph as questioning the virginity of Mary in the conception of Christ, for instance rendering Matthew 1:19 as Joseph resolving "to divorce her quietly" (NAB). This is a simply impossible translation: Nazareth was a small place, and "quiet" divorce would have been impossible. In truth, Joseph never doubted the miraculous nature of Christ's conception, but as a weak man was overwhelmed and wanted to know what his part could possibly be in such a mystery. He wished to withdraw from Mary *out of humility*. He then has his own annunciation in a dream telling him not to fear, for he is to be the guardian of the Redeemer.

Next, Christ is presented in the Temple. This fulfilled the prophecy of Malachi:

> The Lord whom you seek will suddenly come to his temple; the messenger of the covenant in whom you delight, behold, he is coming, says the LORD of hosts. . . . He will sit as a refiner and purifier of silver, and he will purify the sons of Levi and refine them like gold and silver, till they present right offerings to the LORD. (Mal. 3:1, 3)

Again, Christ did not need to be consecrated; instead, in fact, it is He Who completes the consecration of the Temple by fulfilling the power that was only figuratively present in the rites of the Old Law. The Lord of the Temple comes to meet the Temple. He comes not to meet His own needs, nor does Mary, who was also purified in this rite without needing it, but to bring the faith practiced at the Temple to its fulfillment. At this scene we also see Simeon and Anna, who exemplify those who were faithful and just under the Old Law, who looked forward to the consolation of Israel, who spent all their time in fasting and prayer preparing themselves for the Messiah. Christ is that consolation, that fulfillment, that Redeemer. Notice that the prophecy of Simeon proclaims that Jesus, as a tiny child, fulfills the quest of the human race for both the truth of reason in philosophy and faith in the Old Testament: "a light for revelation to the Gentiles [philosophy], and for glory [*shekenah*] to thy people Israel"(Luke 2:32).

The finding in the Temple is an especially important revelation of the person of Christ as wisdom of God. As a child, He is drawn to remain in the Temple and engage the doctors of the Law in discourse. Since His parents sought Him for three days, this must have been a long and interesting exchange. When Mary finds Him, and Jesus responds "How is it that you sought me? Did you not know that I must be in my Father's house?" (Luke 2:49), He is not reproving her. He is merely stating that since they know Who He is, they should not have needed to look for Him for three days. Where else would be He be but in the house of His Father?

Finally, on the cusp of Christ's public ministry, there is His baptism. His entry in the world is completed here, but once again we must remember that Jesus did not need baptism. Jesus came to the waters in a similar way that He came to the Temple: to complete what the waters were made for and as a sign of the true and only baptism in the Holy Spirit, which is baptism in water and His own bloody Passion. These waters will accomplish healing because they will bring the Trinity to us; His touching of them is meant to show that water will now be a means to heal spiritually once He has died on the Cross.

Christ then prays after His baptism not because He needs to, but to show us that His entry in the world is completed by prayer and by listening to Him. Now it has been revealed that He is the beloved Son Who will proclaim the message of God by His words and works. There are some who claim that He needed to hear these words from the Father to understand Who He was at the beginning of His public ministry, but the Gospels never suggest that this manifestation of the Trinity was for Christ's benefit or instruction. Rather, it is for the instruction of the human race.

As we will see, in His way of life in the world, Christ will instruct the world about Who He is — and who we are meant to be — both by word and deed.

10

The Public Ministry

As we said at the very beginning of this book, there are many strange and erroneous ideas about Christ's life and personality out there today. Some people think He was simply a political figure, a revolutionary who fought the Romans. Others think He was, or should have been, a kind of guru or austere holy man, or a carefree hippie. Still others are scandalized by Jesus' all-too-human feelings and passions, preferring to think of Him more like an emotionless android. Lastly there are those who are enticed by the monastic life who think Christ should have lived a solitary life, cut off from the world. After all, according to Catholic tradition, the contemplative way of life is more perfect than the active life. Shouldn't Jesus have just retired to the desert or lived tucked away in an isolated community?

None of these notions really understand Who Christ is and the manner in which He lived in the world. In order to understand why Christ lived the way He did, we have to remember why He took flesh to begin with. He took flesh to redeem us from sin. Christ was a person supremely and totally interested in redeeming people, and that meant being with them and living like them. Everything in the life of Christ was directed toward redemption.

First of all, Christ lived among us so that He might make clear the truth. If He had lived enjoying a peaceful retreat in the desert or mountains, He couldn't have preached the truth to the world. Further, as a good physician of souls He had to seek out the people who needed Him; He couldn't just wait and expect them to come to Him. Finally, Christ took flesh that we might arrive at God. We live in a civilization formed by Christianity, and so we're accustomed to the idea of being raised to godliness, but to the people in the time of Christ this would have been unimaginable. Christ went out to the world, then, so that He could give people confidence to approach God: When they saw the conversion of a tax collector or a centurion, the type widely believed to be unsalvageable, it gave others confidence in His love and mercy. Christ associated with men so that He might show them His divinity through His humanity — by preaching and miracles, and by leading a righteous and blameless life.

Now, it is true that the contemplative life is the most perfect life, absolutely speaking, because it reflects the life of heaven. In heaven we will contemplate God perpetually — this is the ultimate and perfect destiny of humanity. The more perfect life in *this world*, however, is the mixed life of contemplation and action, so that we can take our communion with God and share its fruits with others. We can contemplate God *and* lead others to contemplate Him, too. St Paul said, strikingly, "Woe to me if I do not preach the gospel!" (1 Cor. 9:16).

It is true that Christ did sometimes withdraw to isolated places, but He did this not because He needed to be refreshed in prayer, since He was always in union with the Father, but in order to be an example to those who preach, a reminder that we need to take breaks even from evangelization to feed ourselves spiritually. Similarly, Christ fasted, as we've said, not because He needed to fast but as an example of the kind of sacrifice we can make for the Kingdom. And Christ allowed Himself to be tempted not because He had any fear that He couldn't overcome the temptation but in order to teach us that we will all be tempted, and that God can always bring us through. Christ did all these things to encourage us.

In Christ's day and our own, some have been scandalized that Jesus did not lead a life of greater austerity. The Son of Man enjoyed food and drink and celebrations (just think of the Wedding at Cana) while His forerunner, John the Baptist, ate locusts and wild honey while wearing animal skins in the desert. Meanwhile the only recorded fasting Christ did was during His forty days in the desert before His temptation. And so for some John was the more impressive figure, and Christ a disappointment. The purpose of the Incarnation, however, was that God would associate with men, and in order to associate well with men, He had to conform Himself in reasonable ways to their lifestyles — including appreciating the human pleasures of food and drink and companionship.

This doesn't contradict Christ's perfection because He was perfect in those things that lead us to salvation — that is, matters of the soul. It's not in eating and drinking in themselves that we grow in perfection, but in how we handle abundance and want. Socrates said that the wise man wasn't he who either had much or little, but he who could rejoice without pride in plenty and suffer without despair in lack, and this is quite true. So Christ used food and drink, but He used them for the proper reasons. In truth, both austerity and prosperity, both living apart and living together, can be lawful and useful if one is called to them. Christ taught us that what we must do above all is not conform ourselves to a single model lifestyle but grow in charity and seek the will of God in all states of life.

One must be all things to all men to attract them (see 1 Cor. 9:19–23). So Christ did not condemn fasting but approved both fasting and eating in due moderation. It is not the pain of hunger that gives value to fasting, but the interior integrity it demonstrates and builds. Christ, for example, fasted after His baptism to instruct us that we need penances to live the life of grace. He could have fasted more than forty days, but He did not because He did not want to be an impossible example or lead others to doubt the truth of His humanity.

What about Christ's possessions? It's become trendy to think of poverty and, worse, shabbiness as themselves spiritually elevating, but this isn't quite right. It's true that religious—that is, men and women who vow the evangelical counsels—are called to embrace poverty, and very true that the poor are exalted in the Scripture, but this poverty is not necessarily a physical poverty, but a spirit of detachment. It is also not a forced poverty, but a voluntary one. This spirit *could* be fostered by a lack of material wealth, but there's nothing intrinsically good or attractive in poverty *itself*. If Christ became poor, it was so that it would help Him to promote His mission.

First, if Christ had been too rich He would not have been free to preach. The wealthy man has to spend a great deal of time managing that wealth. Christ, having no property, was free from encumbrance to preach the Gospel. Second, Christ was poor as a sign of contradiction for us: Just as His Death brings spiritual life, so His physical poverty brings spiritual riches. Christ therefore demonstrated physical poverty so that we might be encouraged to seek spiritual riches. Further, in the tradition of other great teachers of the ancient world, Christ charged nothing for His teaching. One of the arguments of Socrates against the Sophists was that he charged nothing for it. As with Socrates so with Christ, this made it clear that His motivation was Truth, not satisfying a paying audience. In the final analysis, Christ neither avoided riches nor sought them; rather He lived with perfect detachment.

One aspect of Christ's preaching that elicits diverging reactions from people was His willingness to challenge, even to offend, His audience. Think of the Bread of Life discourse, when so many followers walked away because they simply couldn't accept what Jesus was telling them. First of all, this shows that the Lord was not just a guru with a simple doctrine of niceness and pacifism. He was not afraid to hurt people's feelings if He knew they could take it and that they needed to hear a given teaching. In Isaiah we read this of the Messiah: "And he will become a sanctuary, and a stone of offense, and a rock of stumbling to both houses of Israel, a trap and a snare to the inhabitants of Jerusalem" (Isa. 8:14). Christ preferred the good and salvation of the many to the serene self-satisfaction of those corrupted by vice who took scandal at His words.

Now, this boldness was in no sense a rebellion of the Lord against legitimate authority. Sometimes people think that the more scandalous they can be in talking about the Faith, the more they're imitating Christ. But Christ's offensiveness wasn't for the sake of giving offense, but to speak the truth while the teachers of Israel were themselves jeopardizing genuine faith. He had a choice between preaching the truth or scandalizing the Pharisees, and He chose the truth. Jesus wished to point out that elders must be respected not based on age or position, but by honesty of life. Additionally, Christ's teaching was, of course, primarily directed to the Jews, but He did not exclude the Gentiles completely because He did not want them to despair. His first convert was, in fact, not a Jew, but the Samaritan Woman.

While Christ gave many teachings publicly, He also said many things privately to the apostles. He obviously did not hide His teaching out of shame or concern for profit, but He was strategic: He progressively revealed the truth to those who were best prepared to accept it. He did not want to expose His teaching to ridicule by those who could not understand it. But for His disciples, He explained everything directly: "To you it has been given to know the secrets of the kingdom of God; but for others they are in parables" (Luke 8:10).

Some find it puzzling that Christ left nothing in writing. People claim Christianity is a religion of the book. This is true because the inspired Scriptures are the source for our understanding of what

Jesus did and taught. Still, the Scriptures were written by inspired authors, not Our Lord, and are determined to be inspired as received and determined by the Church. Jesus wanted to confront every person heart to heart. It is fitting He left nothing in writing because the spoken word is much more powerful and personal than the written word. Even Goebbels, Hitler's propaganda minister knew this. Had Christ left books, people would have spent so much time examining the books that the person of Our Lord would have been lost. This is the way of all great teachers of history: Plato, for example, had to write down what Socrates taught. Also, it is important to remember that in Catholicism, though Scripture is revelation written and inspired, Sacred Tradition came first and is revelation spoken.

Christ also taught through extraordinary revelations of His divinity—that is, through miracles. His miracles generally were not performed just as spectacular displays of personal power or to entice people by extraordinary phenomena. There is some of that, however: Consider the Transfiguration, through which Christ wishes the three apostles to experience the glory of His divinity. But this, as with all His miracles, was done to confirm the truth of His teaching by acts that showed that He possessed the grace of the union of the infirmity of flesh with the power of divinity. In the case of the Transfiguration, for instance, the revelation of the Trinity and His discussion of His Passion with Moses and Elijah were meant to strengthen the apostles for the scandal of the Cross.

It wasn't fitting, however, that Christ should work miracles *before* He taught because it would prime the people to be convinced by power instead of faith and reason. The miracles and the teaching were intertwined, and the moral and intellectual force of those teachings didn't *require* the miraculous to be credible. Further, if His miracles were too early and too fantastic, people might doubt the truth of His humanity.

There has been a tendency, following the Enlightenment, to downplay or even to deny the miracles of Christ. Even His predictions of His Passion and Resurrection are explained away as later additions by the community to make sense of what had happened. Some people, for example, speak of one of Christ's principal miracles, the multiplication of the loaves and the fishes, as merely the miracle of sharing. Jesus did not really feed five thousand people with five loaves and two fish, they say, but rather appealed to the crowds and got them to share their hidden food. Ultimately, this ends up denying that there's anything metaphysical or supernatural about the Gospels.

On the contrary, not only did Christ perform genuine miracles, but He did so in a way unique to Him. There's a big difference between the Lord's miracles and those worked by Old Testament prophets. Christ's miracles surpassed the capacity of all created power, perhaps most notably in actions such as the healing of the man born blind, changing water into wine, and multiplying the loaves. Strikingly, in many of His miracles Christ did not invoke God for the power to perform them.

Consider the difference, for instance, between the way Christ raised the son of the widow at Nain (Luke 7:11–17) and the way Elijah raised the son of a widow (1 Kings 17:17–24). Elijah prayed for an entire day and then placed himself on the boy, and finally God granted Him the favor. Christ simply raises the boy from the dead on His own power and authority, just like that. Christ demonstrates with these miracles that He is the Word Who orders creation, and that creation must obey Him. This is also seen in His power over unclean spirits. He gives orders, and they obey Him. Indeed, they are the first to recognize Who He is: the exorcisms of Christ are essential to the revelation of the mystery of His Person.

The centrality of the miracles of Christ can be seen in what is perhaps the greatest of His miracles: the institution of the Eucharist.

That bread should become human flesh is not in itself so miraculous, since it happens every day through digestion. Of course, that this happens instantaneously at the words of a man is beyond the power of nature. But that it should become God, this is the most miraculous of all. The multiplication of loaves, we should note, rehearses this. The appearances are divided, but all received the same reality. In the Eucharist, the appearances of bread may be broken, but each infinitesimal piece is the entire Body, Blood, soul, and divinity of Christ. We today can participate in this and so be transformed in our souls to adopt Christ's manner of life. The medieval theologians called this, together with the Incarnation, the *miraculum miraculorum* (the miracle of miracles).

In His manner of life in the world, Christ brings us to God to redeem us and to teach us the truth. We can ask with the apostles who witnessed Christ calming the storm on the Sea of Galilee: "What sort of man is this, that even winds and sea obey him?" (Matt. 8:27). And we know the answer.

11

Kenosis and the Cross

Now let us turn to Christ's self-emptying, especially in the context of His agony in the Garden of Gethsemane. In Philippians we read, "Christ Jesus, ... though he was in the form of God, did not count equality with God a thing to be grasped, but emptied himself, taking the form of a servant, being born in the likeness of men" (Phil. 2:5–7). This self-emptying, known in Greek as His *kenosis*, is one of the most beautiful truths about the Savior, but it's also one that has led to confusion. What, exactly, did Christ give up, and what defects did He take on?

Christ's *kenosis* can be defined as the taking of flesh by the Person of the Word to accomplish the atonement. His self-emptying therefore entails lovingly embracing suffering to reverse the unloving disobedience of Adam. Therefore, whatever would compromise this mystery is not fitting for Christ to assume when He takes flesh.

Some think today that the Passion and Death of Christ were regrettable. Jesus could have avoided them had He just been more pluralistic and not so insistent with the authorities about the truth of His identity and message. It is tragic, they say, that His fruitful life was cut so short before its time. On this account, the Passion and Death were not part of Christ's mission, but interruptions of it. Nothing could be further from the truth, however: He took flesh primarily to suffer and die for us.

The first thing to remember, as we've said throughout, is that whatever Christ did, He did not out of necessity for Himself but for our salvation. Simply being capable of suffering was not enough for Him: Since He had to make full satisfaction for our sins, He also had to actually suffer. And the punishment He took upon Himself was the primary and deepest physical punishment for the original sin: death. So Christ had to experience physical pain and emotional desolation, but not any other imperfection that would detract from His loving obedience. And so when it came to Christ's relationship with the Father, His self-emptying did not imply any loss of communion, but rather, as we will soon discuss, the withdrawal of the divine protection that had shielded Jesus during His ministry.

Christ not only satisfied for sin in His sufferings, but He gave us a sign — a sacrament — for our own lives. We don't mean one of the seven sacraments here, but rather an outward sign that shows an inward reality of what our own suffering in the world must be like. By His Death, suffering loss on every level except inner union with God, He taught us to die to materialism and to our powers of manipulation. He was deserted by His friends, was denied by His disciples, had His reputation dragged in the mud by false witness, experienced the tears of His Mother, and suffered pain throughout His entire body. Anyone who has seen the scourging scene in the film the *Passion of the Christ* cannot help but be repulsed by the fact that the hooks lacerated every part of His body, something also witnessed by the Shroud of Turin.

Christ's Death also exemplified perfect virtue. After all: "Greater love has no man than this, that a man lay down his life for his friends" (John 15:13). There is no greater suffering, which in turn requires no greater love, than to endure death without deserving it. Christ also gave us an example of courage, refusing to shrink from justice and truth even in the face of extreme adversity. He showed us of the perfection of patience, teaching us that no matter how deep our sorrow may be, we should not allow it to overwhelm and paralyze us. "My soul is very sorrowful, even to death" (Matt. 26:38).

Christ was never depressed or despairing, though. Perhaps most of all, Christ gave us an example of obedience: the more difficult the precepts obeyed, the more praiseworthy the obedience, and there is no more difficult precept to obey than that of death.

Nowhere except the Cross is Christ's *kenosis* more dramatic, and perhaps puzzling, than in the Garden of Gethsemane. Many have been confused by the Messiah's prayer, "My Father, if it be possible, let this cup pass from me; nevertheless, not as I will, but as thou wilt" (Matt. 26:39). We should be reminded, however, of the text in Hebrews, that Christ "in every respect has been tempted as we are, yet without sinning" (Heb. 4:15). Certainly in the Garden and in the Passion He was tempted by the devil and by the world to abandon His mission of loving obedience due to suffering and sorrow. But Christ's prayer should not be read to mean that He was tempted by His own flesh to turn away from His calling. In us the flesh wars against the spirit, but in Christ they existed in perfect integrity.

Still, does it not appear that Jesus vacillated, at least interiorly, in doing the will of God? But this cannot be, because it would mean He was not perfectly obedient, compromising His satisfaction for our sin. To understand this apparent difficulty further, we have to go back to our discussion of the "levels" of the human will.

Our will is drawn to good in three ways. First of all, it's drawn to the good of the emotions and the senses because these are legitimate and authentic human goods. This is called the *will of sense*. The human will is also drawn to the integrity — that is, the continued existence as an integrated whole — of the person. This is called the *will of nature*. Lastly, the human will is drawn to try to make sense out of competing goods and how they relate to our ultimate good, which is God. This is the *will of choice*.

To some it seems pious, in a way, to say that man is made for death, but this is dangerous. It doesn't make Christ's suffering more heroic to suggest that He acquiesced to death without seeing the

Resurrection, that He threw Himself into the unknown hoping that God might somehow make sense out of the absurdity. It doesn't add to the drama and courage of His Passion to say that Jesus had to suffer the angst of despair or confusion. Many today maintain that even if Christ had the vision of God on earth, in the Passion He reverted to an absurd doubt-filled faith reminiscent of the existentialists of the 1960s.

This attitude cannot be attributed to Christ, and it certainly was not a part of His self-emptying. Christ experienced the Beatific Vision at every moment; He knew about the Resurrection; He knew that man was made for God—and *precisely for this reason* He suffered more in His Passion and Death than any man ever suffered because He understood all that was entailed in sin and thus required in reparation, even though He was blameless. Furthermore, through this Vision He also knew every single individual sin that had been committed or would be committed in the history of the human race, because His atonement was also not only for Original Sin but also for actual sin. He was present to every sin, and it was the horror of the mystery of this wickedness that caused Him such immense interior sorrow.

How could Christ choose this? Returning to the three levels of the will: Christ's human will of sense, which is drawn to the feelings and doesn't immediately participate in the reasonable goods, certainly was repulsed by the suffering He would have to experience. The will of sense simply wants to pursue or avoid experiences because they're delightful or painful. The will of nature, on the other hand, is drawn simply to the survival of the person, but it doesn't distinguish between survival in the eternal sense and survival in the present, worldly sense. In this will, too, Christ would have been repulsed by what was to happen to Him. Neither of these levels of the will, though, is the deepest manner of human willing, nor is either the place where real choice takes place.

Our genuinely free will is the choosing will. In free will, we look at various means and judge whether these means in fact serve the ultimate good. Christ, in order to suffer in true obedience, had to examine and judge all the various goods and evils that were presented before Him and, using that choosing will, make a decision that it was better to suffer than not to suffer. His prayer in the Garden asking if it was possible not to suffer did not mean that He vacillated in His purpose or His mission; it meant, rather, that He genuinely inquired with His Father whether a different *means* to that final end was possible.

Christ's self-emptying can never mean that He lost His communion with God, either by grace or by vision. We often enter doubtfully into our choices because of the limitations of sense knowledge, because we don't yet see the whole picture as God sees it, both in terms of morality and reality. But Christ had no such limitations. He was not limited by interior weakness nor by ignorance of the final and full human destiny in perfect communion with God. However, by His will He did not allow the glory of His perfect vision of God to penetrate into His emotions and body: In this sense He was still genuinely a pilgrim with us. His body and emotions were not yet at the end, even while His soul was. He does not let Himself, you could say, pre-experience the glory of the Resurrection. He only merits that in justice by His obedience. "No one takes my life from me; I have power to lay it down and take it up again" (see John 10:18).

Though it's true that Christ could not sin in the sense that He could not turn aside from the vision of God, He did have to exercise human choice over and over again in determining what that vision demanded of Him in particular circumstances. Thus, even though the will of sense and the will of nature might be repulsed by something that was presented to Him, Christ's choosing was never deflected or distracted from His mission. There was no *actual* conflict between Christ, on one level, fleeing from the suffering of the Cross and, and on the other level, truly and fully and freely embracing it.

Remember the example of the gangrenous hand: We can be repulsed by a dangerous and painful life-saving operation and still choose it freely because the choosing will recognizes the higher good, saving our life. We can see how this works quite clearly in that famous prayer of Christ in the Garden. Going back to Matthew 26:39, we recognize that the first clause — "My Father, if it be possible, let this cup pass from me" — comes from the wills of sense and nature, abhorring the pain to come. But the second clause — "nevertheless, not as I will, but as thou wilt" — comes from the choosing will, and Christ freely hands His will over to His Father's, never vacillating in that for a moment. Rather than demonstrating fear of hesitation, this prayer proves the total patience, the total obedience, the total love, and the total courage of Christ.

He examined in His reason everything that was placed before Him — including His own feelings. We should note that the Father in no sense wanted Christ to deny His human feelings as though He weren't afraid. The courageous person is not the one who doesn't feel fear. That's rash and often irrational. Rather, the courageous person is one who shows his inner integrity by choosing the just, right, and good thing even in face of intense fear. Christ, on the level of His reason and judgment, without vacillation and without doubt and without hesitation, gives us a perfect example of this, as He judged it simply better, knowing all the costs, to be obedient to the Father.

In fact, God wanted to preserve Christ's human resistance to suffering to show that the will of sense and the will of nature are not meant to compromise the divine will or the choosing will. There was no contradiction in the natures of Christ, as there should not be within our souls in their relationship with God, but rather an intense communion among all aspects of His person. So in thinking about Christ's self-emptying, which is most perfectly witnessed in His agony, Passion, and Death, we have to affirm once again that it never involves breaking communion with His Father, or the hypostatic union within Himself. Jesus is always the person of the Word shown to us in human form and nature. Once He takes this upon Himself it is a permanent personal union.

At the same time and in the same person, Christ enjoyed a genuine earthly pilgrimage in His body and emotions and, with the higher part of His intelligence, was continually moved by God for His purposes: the God Whom He saw in every moment, the God Who He was. Thus He saw how all of creation and all of Providence related to the final destiny of the human race joined back to God in heaven. And He could choose to play His part.

"My God, my God, why hast thou forsaken me?" (Ps. 22:1; Matt. 27:46). Many people, from ancient heretics to modern theologians, have seen in this cry of Christ on the Cross a proof that Jesus must have been just like any other human being, that He must have suffered interior weakness, hopelessness, and angst, that He must have lost the Beatific Vision and His awareness that He was going to rise from the dead. In that moment, they say, His Messiahship must have seemed like just a dream.

Great heresies always accept one extreme and, in so doing, exclude some other truth. So many have stressed Christ's divinity at the expense of His humanity, or His humanity at the expense of His divinity. It is necessary, however, for us to affirm *both* that Christ experienced the Beatific Vision while on the Cross *and* that He truly and fully drank the cup God willed for Him. Christ's agony and pain must be completely affirmed at the same time as His possession of perfect happiness. It is not a question of either-or; with Christ, it is always *both*. It is the attempt to distinguish absolutely between Christ's divinity and His human will, or to deny one or the other, which has led to so many difficulties.

Christ's self-emptying on the Cross, and His cry that His Father has "forsaken" Him, cannot mean that the Word was abandoned in His person. As we've said, the divine communion in Christ is unbreakable. Therefore, it must be understood through the lens of this absolute communion. We can see this in the manner in which Christ Himself approached His own emptying. As we know, Christ did not allow the glory of His divinity to enter into His emotions and His body. His perfectly infused reason, present to the Father, in no sense reduced the emotional and physical pain of His Passion. That which is absolutely reasonable is not, contra *Star Trek* and Mr. Spock, absolutely emotionless. Rather, perfect integrity means the *elevation* of feeling to its highest heights *along with* reason. Virtue does not reduce feeling; virtue increases it. Christ by His own will allowed none of the joy in His higher self to overflow into His emotions so that He might drink fully of the cup of suffering. He allowed no mitigation of the Passion.

"My God, my God, why hast thou forsaken me?" (Ps. 22:1; Matt. 27:46). These words cannot refer to God forsaking His Son by withdrawing either His divine personhood or His communion or His grace or the Vision of God that He possessed from the moment of His conception in His human mind. In fact, these words are from a psalm, Psalm 22, which would have been known to the Jewish observers of the Crucifixion.

Many pious men through history have thought that Christ continued to recite this psalm in silence—and it is not a psalm of despair, but rather one of triumph, of supreme confidence in God in the face of suffering. The divine forsaking described in the first lines is not a real abandonment, but rather a poetical expression from a person who suffers from severe and unremitting physical pain, as we know Christ did. God's abandonment of the psalmist is *apparent* but not complete: He never turns His face away from the psalmist's—or certainly Christ's—true interior life. In making this prayer of pain, Christ shows that His body is not yet glorified, not yet free from human frailty, and that for love of us He doesn't want it to be.

Let us read further in this psalm:

> For he has not despised or abhorred
> the affliction of the afflicted;
> and he has not hid his face from him,
> but has heard, when he cried to him.
> From thee comes my praise in the great congregation;
> my vows I will pay before those who fear him.
> The afflicted shall eat and be satisfied;
> those who seek him shall praise the LORD!
> May your hearts live for ever!...
> Posterity shall serve him;
> men shall tell of the Lord to the coming generation,
> and proclaim his deliverance to a people yet unborn,
> that he has wrought it. (Ps. 22:24–26, 30–31)

It is clear that the psalmist is not questioning or rebuking the Lord, but rather praising His goodness and mercy. Despite intense suffering, the psalmist has confidence that God is with Him and will resolve His troubles. In praying this psalm, Christ was not a victim in the hands of unfeeling Providence, but a person Who in His humanity was embracing the suffering God gave Him and expressing confidence in its final and perfect resolution. A moment later in Matthew's Passion, we read, "And Jesus cried again with a loud voice and yielded up his spirit" (Matt. 27:50). Traditionally, spiritual authors have interpreted this to mean that Jesus voluntarily embraced His Death. Remember: "No one takes [my life] from me, but I lay it down of my own accord" (John 10:18).

Christ's *kenosis*—His self-emptying—did not consist in losing anything of God within Himself. But it did involve losing something from the Father: His protection. Multiple times in the Gospels Jesus said, "My hour has not yet come," (see John 2:4) signifying that it was not yet time for God's will for Him—including the withdrawal of divine protection—to be fulfilled. We can see this protection when Jesus visited Nazareth and was rejected by His own neighbors:

> And they rose up and put him out of the city, and led him to the brow of the hill on which their city was built, that they might throw him down headlong. But passing through the midst of them he went away. (Luke 4:29–30)

It was not yet Christ's hour, and so God facilitated His escape from the mob. But, when Christ's time did come, when the moment of our redemption was at hand, God withdrew His protection so that it might be fulfilled. But He never withdraw His communion.

Many times we experience our own share in the Passion. Ours is lived in faith; Christ's in vision. Nevertheless, the merits of His Passion and Death always support us in our own suffering. "With his stripes we are healed" (Isa. 53:5).

12

He Is Risen

When Pilate showed the bloodied Christ crowned with thorns to the people, he said, "*Ecce Homo*" — "Behold the Man." In so doing, he was unknowingly telling the crowd to regard what we do to one another as a result of Original Sin. As the serpent Moses lifted up in the desert was a sign of the disease from which the Israelites suffered, so Christ lifted up on the Cross shows us what lust, domination, and manipulation do to us. Jesus is humiliated physically by our spiritual disease, by our ignorance, weakness, malice, and lust.

From His Passion, we see what our sin has wrought upon ourselves — that is, what kind of suffering we must undergo. But this is not the end of the story. "And being found in human form he humbled himself and became obedient unto death, even death on a cross. *Therefore God has highly exalted him...*" (Phil. 2:8–9, emphasis added). In His exaltation, we see the resolution of His Death on the Cross; we see that once sin is defeated we are given hope in our final destiny. In Christ's triumph over death, He shows us what we are really bound for — that same Beatific Vision that He experiences perpetually. By His perfect obedience on the Cross, He merited His own Resurrection for Himself, but also for us: The glory He experienced was a perfect completion of what the life of man should be on earth. Christ's Resurrection is the solution to the problem of man posed by His dual nature.

This exaltation begins with what is traditionally called "the harrowing of hell." Right there in the Apostles' Creed we say that Christ "descended into hell." This occurred during the three days His body lay in the tomb. Meanwhile, His human soul entered what is called the limbo of the just — the place where all those who had received grace by their faith in the future Messiah waited for the one Whom they saw from afar. As Christ preached three years on earth, He now preached three days in limbo, also known as Sheol or Hades by the ancients. "The gospel was preached even to the dead" (1 Pet. 4:6).

There is a beautiful painting by Fra Angelico that depicts the Lord, holding the banner of Resurrection, breaking into hell while all the saints of the Old Testament rush to Him. They now understand fully the one in Whom they believed with implicit faith. This adds to Satan's suffering. The *Catechism* quotes an ancient homily for Holy Saturday:

> He has gone to search for Adam, our first father, as for a lost sheep. Greatly desiring to visit those who live in darkness and in the shadow of death, he has gone to free from sorrow Adam in his bonds and Eve, captive with him — He who is both their God and the son of Eve. (635)

When Christ rises from the tomb, He brings these people to heaven.

Just as Pilate's *"Ecce Homo"* shows the painful and horrible limitations of fallen human nature after the original sin, when the Risen Jesus appears in the Upper Room and wishes the apostles "peace," He demonstrates what man is really meant to be. Man is a unity of body *and* soul in absolute unity. Our immortal soul is not an accessory, our God-seeking intellect not an optional add-on to our humanity. This means that man is a being made for God, not a being made for death. Death is, in every sense of the word, *unnatural* for man considered as a whole. Yes, the body considered in itself tends to death. Our material powers have nothing within themselves that can keep them alive forever. But the body is not just an abstraction from the soul; the two are intrinsically connected. So the person, taken as a whole, is made for heaven because man's nature is made up of both body and soul.

The problem of man demonstrates that the body cannot be dead forever while the soul lives forever. The pre-Christian philosopher Aristotle figured out that the soul was immortal. His predecessor, Plato, resolved the problem of a finite body attached to an eternal soul by saying that the body is an illusion. For Aristotle, on the other hand, the body was just as much a part of the whole person as the soul. The problem of death is simply that all bodies die, but if the soul lives forever, then it should be — and is — impossible for the body to remain dead forever. It's an unnatural condition, and no unnatural condition can endure forever.

Before the first sin, Adam could have died, but it would have been an instantaneous separation of his soul from his body, without corruption or violence, more like a falling asleep followed by an instantaneous resurrection. This is because God preserved the body of the first man from suffering and a decaying death, as would later be the case with the body of Mary. After the sin, however, we all know there's nothing internal to the body that can prevent it from dying, and that death is always in some sense violent, and (nearly) always followed by corruption.

But on the third day after His Death, Christ brought resurrection to man again. By the miraculous power of God, man was not only freed from the permanence of death. The problem of man — the composite of an immortal soul with a mortal body — was resolved. Now not only the soul but also the body can — and must — participate in divine transcendent life. Our bodies live again and cannot again die. When Christ appears in the Upper Room and shows the disciples His hands and feet He is saying now, as Pilate did only a few days prior: "*Ecce Homo.*" This is not what man is, but what man should be and will be.

Sadly, there are Catholic thinkers today who maintain that the Resurrection of Jesus did not involve either His flesh rising again or the corporal experience of His body by His friends. His exaltation, they say, was one of wishful thinking created by the Church, which needed to make sense of the Passion. Some say there is no objective experience of the risen body of Christ except His appearance to St. Paul on the road to Damascus which, of course, entailed no physical touching.

This is contrary to both faith and reason. It is true the Resurrection of Jesus is a mysterious and transcendent event. But the Church has always proclaimed it is also a historical one. The *Catechism* is clear: "Given all these testimonies, Christ's Resurrection cannot be interpreted as something outside the physical order, and it is impossible not to acknowledge it as an historical fact" (643). The idea that this is not the case is due to a problematic philosophy of subjectivity, which says that truth is created by and through each individual's experience, and which has become distressingly prevalent in our contemporary Church. Christ is risen, on this account, only because the disciples' faith conjured the idea into being. Again, however, the *Catechism* is clear:

> Therefore the hypothesis that the Resurrection was produced by the apostles' faith (credulity) will not hold up. On the contrary, their faith in the Resurrection was born, under the action of divine grace, from their direct experience of the reality of the risen Jesus. (644)

Now, what kind of body did Christ take upon Himself in His exaltation? It wasn't a ghostly body, but it was, in a certain sense, a spiritualized body. Mostly, though, the Lord took upon Himself

His own body—a real fleshly body, with all of its original powers. He demonstrated this quite dramatically to Thomas when He invited the doubting apostle to put his finger in His wounds. More prosaically, Christ demonstrated the corporal reality of His body by eating a piece of fish with the apostles. But His resurrected body did have some special spiritual powers, such as the ability to pass through walls, as when He appeared in the Upper Room.

Let's consider a few final issues concerning the Resurrection. First, it is true that Christ could have arisen immediately after His Death; He was under no obligation to wait three days, though it did fulfill the Old Testament prophecies. More practically: if He rose too quickly, it might have seemed that He never died at all and therefore didn't rise to a new way of existing. Then there's the question of *Who* exactly raised Jesus. Sometimes Christ's Resurrection is attributed to the Father and sometimes to Christ Himself, but in truth there's no contradiction here. As man, Christ merited the divine power, which is divine power whether it's from the Father, the Son, or the Holy Spirit. The important thing is that His body was brought back to life and had a new relationship with His soul such that it perfectly and spontaneously obeyed the soul—including powers of movement that would be impossible for a body limited by time and space. In this, Christ does away with the mortality of the body; His body becomes unable to die, and so will ours.

During His earthly life and ministry Christ did not allow the glory of the Beatific Vision to overflow into His body. Now they literally surged through His emotions and through His flesh. Christ did this to anticipate the general resurrection, to give us a beautiful and hopeful vision while we're on earth of what our true destiny and happiness is. To the suffering, Christ wishes to show us that there will be a final and perfect resolution to our existence, provided we rely on Him to maintain the integrity of our souls. He demonstrates with His glorified body that the fullness of human nature is not found in earthly happiness, but in the absolute integrity of our flesh with our spirit when we see God face to face.

To this end Jesus appeared on earth for forty days after His Resurrection to instruct His apostles with the evidence of His risen body, showing the true and final character of human life to our dull minds. Remember the Road to Emmaus: Here are disciples who had lived with the Lord and witnessed His Death, and He walked with them in His risen body for several hours, instructing them in the Scriptures and trying to show them how everything pointed to the Resurrection, and still they don't understand. Only when He performs an act of intimacy with them — breaking bread — are their minds opened. How dull we often are in the midst of our sufferings, blinded by our own pain, self-centeredness, and impatience, not recognizing what is possible for us and what we're really made for.

Christ's Ascension was also fitting, first because His glorified body could not die, but also as an act of justice, because He was humiliated in two ways. First, He was humiliated by suffering and death, which was resolved in His Resurrection. Then, He was also humiliated by spending time in the grave, and this is restored in justice by His Ascension into heaven. This Ascension befits His human nature, while sitting at the right hand of the Father befits His divine nature. From heaven, He again shows us what humanity is made for.

The Ascension should not be considered something remote from us, and certainly not an abandonment. In the Holy Mass, in fact, we enter into heaven with Christ. The same Body, Blood, Soul, and Divinity now becomes present on the altar during each and every Mass. Christ offers Himself anew, not detracting from His original bloody sacrifice but making the fruits of that sacrifice present as the Mediator between God and man. The priest and victim of the Passion are united with Christ resurrected and ascended in His exaltation. St. Augustine says: "The priest is the same, the victim is the same, only the manner of offering differs."

In the great entrance into this priestly act, which is the Eucharistic Prayer or Canon, we unite ourselves to the heavenly worship in the adoration of the mystic Lamb described in the book of Revelation. All the heavenly court, and indeed the entire cosmos, worships. We participate in that worship when we say: "Holy, holy, holy, Lord God of hosts." At Mass, indeed each time we celebrate the sacraments, He becomes present, and all the angels rejoice. "It is in this eternal liturgy that the Spirit and the Church enable us to participate whenever we celebrate the mystery of salvation in the sacraments" (*Catechism of the Catholic Church*, 1139).

In man there are two deaths: the death of the body and the death of the soul. Christ did not experience the second, which is sin. But He did experience the first, and through it and for us He destroyed both deaths. There is also a twofold life. There is the life of the body imparted by the soul; this is the life given to us by nature. There is also the life of the soul imparted to us by grace and justice. Christ, in His Resurrection, gave to us the resurrection of body and soul, together, forever.

"For Christ, our paschal lamb, has been sacrificed. Let us, therefore, celebrate the festival" (1 Cor. 5:7–8). Christ has risen for us; therefore we must have hope in our own resurrection. And Christ stands before us as a sacrament and sign of our resurrection, to show us that our life in the Holy Spirit, which He gives us here on earth, is only completed in heaven.

13

The Savior Is Exalted

Men of Galilee, why do you stand looking into heaven? This Jesus, who was taken up from you into heaven, will come in the same way as you saw him go into heaven. (Acts 1:11)

These are the words of the angels to the apostles after Christ's Ascension—the final and fullest exaltation of His human body after the humiliation of His earthly sojourn, from the judgment of wicked men to His suffering, Death, and three days in the grave. His divine nature, of course, had always been exalted, since before the creation of the world. In heaven, Christ received His role to be the standard by which all human life is judged. In His exaltation at the right hand of the Father, He executes divine power and authority in His office as judge.

"Every eye will see him, every one who pierced him; and all tribes of the earth will wail on account of him" (Rev. 1:7). When all men come before Him, Christ in His glorious form—with His wounds still in evidence—will pronounce the sentence for their lives. Those wounds, though, will not be a *disfigurement* of His flesh; rather they will shine gloriously because it is by them that He has truly and finally atoned for our sins.

We will all experience two judgments. The first is a particular judgment when Christ judges us worthy of heaven or hell. The souls in purgatory have already been judged worthy of heaven but cannot yet enter until they have passively atoned for the temporal punishment that remains from sin. The souls of the just then enter heaven, and they see God directly without any mediation whatsoever. The light of the eternal God fills their minds. Freedom and nature come to a perfect fulfillment in them. The souls of the damned, on the other hand, enter hell. They are eternally deprived of the vision of God Who alone can fulfill the power of the intellect. Freedom and nature forever conflict within them, and so they will suffer the deepest frustration and the deepest pain.

This particular judgment, though, is not the final consummation. There is still something missing. All throughout this book, we have emphasized the fact that the body and the soul make up the substance of man. In the particular judgment, the soul is either satisfied or not. The body, however, must participate in this for man to be naturally complete. This happens in the general judgment at the end of time. In this judgment, described in Matthew 25:31–46, the Son of Man will separate the sheep from the goats and judgment will be pronounced by the mouth of the Lord. All hidden deeds will be made known before the entirety of assembled creation. The bodies of the dead will rise, and the good will have glorified bodies filled with light and agility while the wicked will have immortal bodies filled with pain and darkness. The announcement of what is hidden in the soul will add to the glory of the blessed and the suffering of the damned. The standard of judgment will be how closely each person had imitated Christ: Works do not merit grace, but man is expected to cooperate with grace already received through works. The principle of merit in heaven, then, will be how much one has loved God on earth.

How do we prepare for this judgment? "Watch therefore, for you know neither the day nor the hour" (Matt. 25:13). We watch by living a life of virtue, by keeping our eyes on the Lord, and especially by prayer—a life of mystical union with the God of mystical love. Our life on earth, then, becomes an imitation of His Passion, one continuous dying to self. This does not come to pass by our own power, however, but by the atoning power that He wrought as our priest and mediator. His atonement is sustained in us because, through His grace, the Trinity comes again in intimacy to live in our souls so that we can move toward our true goal, heaven. In the last chapter, we discussed how this is nourished by the sacraments, and especially the Eucharist. This is because after the Incarnation, we can only experience the love of the Holy Spirit in the soul through the physical mission of Christ in the flesh. The priesthood of Christ is an expression of this.

As high priest, Christ, by His Death, satisfied for sin, and by His Resurrection, He gives us the gift of new heavenly life. Both of these realities are seen in His risen body at the right hand of the Father, where His obedient sacrifice is fully accepted for our disobedience. This obedience must, in turn, come to define our daily lives. This isn't about extraordinary actions or visions, but about growing progressively in trust and faith in God in the most ordinary things that we do. The most important moments are those little, unobtrusive acts of patience — with our fellow men and with the world around us — by which we form our attitudes and our souls in Christ. Thus we show ourselves and others that our souls are being exalted in God. We preserve this exaltation, then, only through union with His Body and Blood in the Eucharist.

Christ now lives at the right hand of the Father with the marks of His wounds as a sign of His accepted sacrifice, and the attitude of His sacrifice must become our own. It is in the Eucharist and the Mass that we enter most deeply into Christ's life, Passion, Death, Resurrection, and exaltation. When the priest pronounces the words of institution over the host, that same body that was generated in the womb of Our Lady, that walked and talked on this earth, that performed miracles, that died on the Cross, and that is now risen in Heaven, with all the atoning merit and motivation that was present in Christ's human will, becomes present to us. When we receive Him in Communion, our bodies mingle with His as a preparation for our own resurrection.

Christ is said to be a high priest forever after the order of Melchizedek (see Ps. 110:4). We could devote an entire book to Melchizedek and his priesthood, but let us make just a few points here. First, Melchizedek is said to have had no mother or father. The Jews interpreted this to mean that his priesthood was eternal, and so is Christ's. Second, the sacrifice of Melchizedek was a sacrifice made with bread and wine, just like the sacrifice of the Eucharist. Third, Melchizedek received tithes from Abraham, who was regarded by the Jews as representing the Levitical priesthood. Thus in tying Christ to Melchizedek, His priesthood is shown to be more powerful than the Levitical priesthood.

Now some have taken this doctrine as in some way denigrating the singular bloody sacrifice of Christ on the Cross, but this isn't the case at all. The fruits of the sacrifice on Calvary are indeed eternal and infinite. But they become applied to each of us in our own time and place in the Sacrifice of the Mass, where we enter and participate in Christ's sacrifice, which becomes present in a new way for us. Indeed the separation of the bread and wine has often been taken as a sign of the separation at Christ's Death between His body and soul. He is the priest *and* the victim, and we become a part of His priesthood *and* a part of His offering.

This sacrifice fulfills completely the three principal kinds of sacrifice in the Old Law. First, sacrifice was a sin offering. By Christ's obedience on the Cross, He reverses our own disobedience. Second, sacrifice was a peace offering. Christ by His sacrifice brings to us again the ability to enter into intimate union with the Trinity. Further, He allows us to nourish that union in our souls because His sacrifice makes available the sanctifying grace that preserves our peace with God. And the third type of sacrifice of the Old Law was the holocaust, the complete destruction of the victim to demonstrate the giving of oneself completely to God. Christ shows that man can lose everything, provided He does not lose His interior union and integrity with God, which is what it means to be truly human.

Because of Christ's sacrifice, and because of the nourishment He provides in the Holy Eucharist and the Sacrifice of the Mass, we can now cry confidently, "Abba Father!" We can now experience and nourish the daily intimacy with God that must permeate all of our actions. In other words, we who are here on earth must daily enter into all that is contained in Christ's atonement. This is, first of all, the removal of sin through the grace of interior justification from, and communion with, the Holy Spirit. Secondly, as part of this restoration of grace, Christ's atonement ends our liability to punishment for Adam's sin. Christ has instead taken all the punishment upon Himself, and now He sits at the right hand of the Father. Thus, when we enter into Him through the Sacrifice of the Mass, that punishment is finally and truly resolved. Returning to First Corinthians: "For Christ, our paschal lamb, has been sacrificed. Let us, therefore, celebrate the festival…with the unleavened bread of sincerity and truth" (1 Cor. 5:7–8).

As we enter into this union with Christ's Body and His very Person, His prayer life, obedience, and union with God should become our own. Grace is what gives us the ability to do this, and we can only understand and cooperate with this grace to the extent that we sacrifice ourselves as He did. The "unleavened bread of sincerity and truth" means that with sincerity we look upon God with an undivided heart, and in truth we contemplate Him as our faith dictates.

And so we turn one last time to the question: Who is Jesus Christ? Perhaps the most important single sentence in Scripture to answer this is in First Timothy: "For there is one God, and there is one mediator between God and men, the man Christ Jesus" (1 Tim. 2:5). In

His human nature, He is separated from God, and yet in His human nature He is more human—more eminent in grace and glory—than all other human beings. In His human nature He presents to us divine gifts and He atones for our sin, which is nothing less than the fulfillment of the mission of Christ.

The revelation of the Trinity can be expressed in "missions" that reflect the inner relationship of each Person to the Triune God. The Father has no mission, but sends the other two in mission. The Son, on the other hand, has both an invisible and visible mission. As the Word begotten by the Father, He is the Truth; in the flesh He takes from Mary He brings mankind back to the Truth lost in Original Sin. These were His missions on earth, and they remain His missions in heaven. In the Upper Room, the Lord completes His prayer by saying to the Father: "Sanctify them in the truth; thy word is truth" (John 17:17).

Later, He breathes on the apostles, saying, "Receive the Holy Spirit" (John 20:22). This is the origin of the invisible mission of the Holy Spirit, Who is sent by both the Father and the Son, hence exhalation from the Lord's body. The Ancient Fathers called the Holy Spirit the *osculum suavissimum*, the most sweet kiss of the Father and the Son, because He proceeds from both after the manner of love. Like the Son, He has two missions: His invisible mission is our holiness, and His visible mission is symbolized in the dove, the wind, and the tongues of fire. The sacramental order reflects the visible mission of the Son, which is now necessary for all eternity for our holiness in the Spirit. There can be no spiritual Church apart from the sacramental Church.

Let us reiterate that Christ cannot be separated between the Jesus of faith and the Jesus of history, or the Christ from above and the Christ from below. These artificial distinctions do injustice to Who He really is. When the apostles experienced Christ's humanity through their senses, they experienced the Divine Person of the

Word, and because the Word is united with the other Persons of the Trinity in one nature, they also experienced His divine nature. In other words, in the most ordinary things of life they experienced the Divine Person of the Word. To try to conjure distinct versions of Jesus Christ is to suggest that His human nature can be separated from His Divine Person.

Christ was also not just a good man who has become identified with God. Christ always existed as God, as the second Person of the Trinity with the divine nature. He began to exist with a human nature in the womb of His mother. It is not God Who has changed; it is creation that has changed. The doctrine of Christ was not something that people learned simply by osmosis, and it was not arbitrary or irrational. They learned it, as we do in the sacraments, from and through Him. This reality was and is the very truth of the inner mystery of the life of the Trinity itself, which is both perfect love and perfect reason. In that doctrine, we are all instructed that through the actions of His body we can all be reunited with the God Who is our all.

While Christ performed miracles, which are extremely important to understanding His mission, the primary way He atoned for us was by the simple goodness of a human will filled with the divine presence of the Trinity. Here on earth, He invites us to discover our share in His divine nature through the means of His human nature—to associate ourselves with Him in all that He is and all that He has been, from His birth to His ministry to His Passion, Death, and exaltation, and through Him to find the means by which we return to the God Who created us. When we experience the Lord Jesus in His human nature on earth, we are really entering into God.

Christ prays for us. He is our priest. In Him we return back to the God from Whom we came. By the grace that granted Him the Beatific Vision and union with God the Father, and by the grace that made Him a perfectly justified human being, Christ's human nature is the channel by which we can enter into prayer and intimacy with God again. Through the capital grace, as our one true high priest and mediator He wants us to give ourselves, in the ordinary things of life, continuously and always to Him. For this grace, we pray to Him because He is our Lord.

> Though he was in the form of God, [Christ Jesus] did not count equality with God a thing to be grasped, but emptied himself, taking the form of a servant, being born in the likeness of men. And being found in human form he humbled himself and became obedient unto death, even death on a cross. Therefore God has highly exalted him and bestowed on him the name which is above every name, that at the name of Jesus every knee should bow, in heaven and on earth and under the earth, and every tongue confess that Jesus Christ is Lord, to the glory of God the Father. (Phil. 2:6–11)

This beautiful hymn from Philippians perfectly summarizes the lessons I aimed to teach in this book. The Lord emptied Himself; the Lord suffered death; the Lord was exalted; and in all of this nothing about Him was changed, except how we came to know Him once He took flesh. It wasn't that He became "more" God in His Incarnation, and it wasn't that He merited any more than He always had. It was, rather, that He gave, and gives, His grace to us.

About the Author

Fr. Brian Thomas Becket Mullady is the son of an Air Force officer and was raised throughout the United States. He entered the Dominican Order in 1966 and was ordained in Oakland, California, in 1972. He has been a parish priest, high school teacher, retreat master, mission preacher, and university professor. He received his doctorate in sacred theology (STD) from the Angelicum University in Rome and was a professor there for six years. He has taught at several colleges and seminaries in the United States. He is currently a mission preacher and retreat master for the Western Dominican Province. He also teaches two months of the year at Holy Apostles Seminary in Cromwell, Connecticut. Fr. Mullady has had fourteen series on the EWTN Global Catholic Network. He is the author of four books and numerous articles and writes the answer column in *Homiletic and Pastoral Review*. He is also designated as an official Missionary of Mercy by Pope Francis.